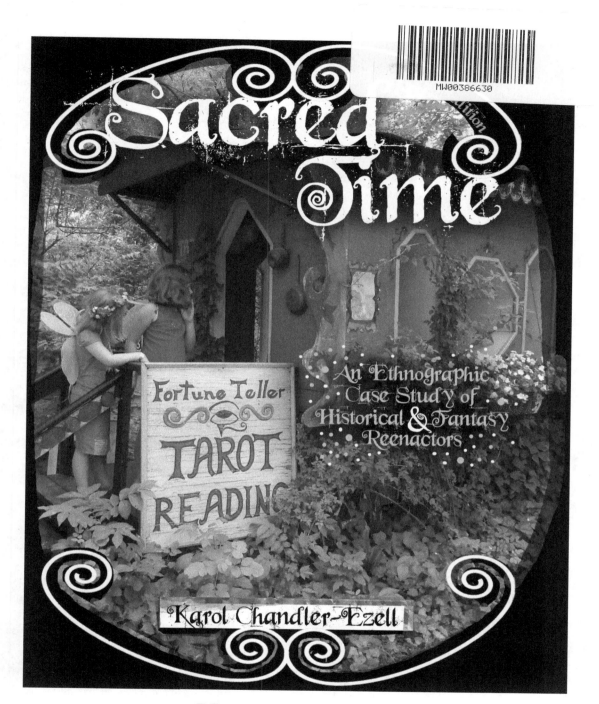

Sacred Time

An Ethnographic Case Study of Historical & Fantasy Reenactors

Fortune Teller
TAROT READING

Karol Chandler-Ezell

Kendall Hunt
publishing company

Cover images courtesy of Karol Chandler-Ezell

Kendall Hunt
p u b l i s h i n g   c o m p a n y
www.kendallhunt.com
Send all inquiries to:
4050 Westmark Drive
Dubuque, IA 52004-1840

Table of Contents

Preface

Goals and Themes of this Book

Sacred Time is intended to provide an approachable ethnographic study of historical reenactors. The first two editions were published as *Historical Reenactors and "the Period Rush": The Cultural Anthropology of Paracultures*, but after nearly a decade of teaching about reenactors and continuing to study and reflect on them, the book needed substantial revision and updating. This third edition includes the influence of my students at Stephen F. Austin State University and my colleagues over the years. In being forced to try to find ways to explain reenacting, paracultures, and the ever-evolving nature of culture to my students, I've re-interpreted this ethnography as well. It is hopefully more readable and presented with greater clarity that does justice to the reader and the reenactors who inspired it.

    Sacred Time presents an anthropological look at reenactment groups and the people who participate in them. The book has three objectives. First, this is an anthropological investigation of reenactment groups that explores the activities and motivations of participants. I take a bio-cultural and adaptive approach to this study, asking "why do people participate in reenacting?" and "what function does it serve?" To answer these questions, I apply sociocultural theories of adaptive behavior, cultural function, social movements, and cultural processes to understand the role that reenactment participation plays for individuals. Society for Creative Anachronism, Renaissance Faire, Civil War, and other reenactment groups are described and discussed. The groups are compared and contrasted to better understand both the similarities and differences among the groups. Though the SCA and other medieval European groups are not the most common or oldest of the reenactors, as the first group I investigated, they are the standard to which I began to compare other groups.

    Second, this book allows me to present information gathered during my dissertation research into the use of herbal remedies by Americans. In my search for individuals using and practicing traditional European herbal medicine, I found that many people were using and studying traditional or folk medicine as a part of historical reenactment activities. In particular, many members of the Society for Creative Anachronism (SCA) were very knowledgeable about medieval European medicine. Many of the experts I initially discovered actually suggested I come to reenactment events and meetings to watch them in action and meet other informants. In this way, I learned that the rediscovery and sharing of historical knowledge is a very important part of reenactment culture. In order to access and interview herbal medicine use, I needed to do ethnographic work with historical reenactment groups. Many of the herbal practitioners and consumers I interviewed were involved in alternative groups and had multiple social connections to historical and/or fantasy reenactors even if they themselves did not participate. The underlying network of social connections was linked through the reenactment and other social groups, not the herbal knowledge use itself. I began by studying the culture of herbal remedies and ended by learning that herbal remedy knowledge was actually a manifestation of deeper cultural movements like establishing and maintaining a connection to historical, cultural, and environmental heritage. Use of herbal and other alternative medicines by these people was revealed as a symptom of social problems and unmet needs in American culture that people were solving through revitalization movements. As I tried to learn more about reenactors and better understand how they were connected to my dissertation topic, I realized that these groups were largely unstudied. This book is an attempt to share the world of paracultures and the people who inhabit these realms.

Third, *Sacred Time* illustrates the ethnographic and ethnobiological research process. I use this book and the topic of reenacting to illustrate broader anthropological and social concepts about culture's adaptive nature and how cultural movements are shaped by peoples' needs.

I have written this book to be accessible to undergraduate students and beginning living history and interpretation graduate students in the social sciences as well as those who have an interest in reenactment groups. I hope that it will also interest professionals and more advanced graduate students interested in social movements, social psychology, and culture change.

Organization

The book is arranged in 3 parts. Part I: Chapters 1–4, provides an overview of the project, basic terms and concepts, and the basic ethnographic methods used to study historic reenactment groups. Part II describes and compares the reenactment groups ethnographically in Chapters 5, 6, and 7. Finally, in Part III: Chapters 8 and 9 revisit the theoretical concepts, placing the reenactors in a larger context to demonstrate what they reveal about culture and our social needs. Each chapter has a set of suggested assignments or activities students may use to learn more.

Acknowledgements

I would like to acknowledge the people who have contributed to this work and without whom this book would not exist. First, I would like to thank all of the reenactors who gave generously of their time and knowledge. They welcomed me and brought me into their world. Kristina Hayen served as my guide into the SCA, introducing me to the art of "playing" and other reenactors, undertaking my initial enculturation, and even hosting me at events. My thanks to Kris, Damon Lotz, Mike Hill, and the friendly reenactors I met in their company for helping to welcome me to the SCA world. My gratitude to the many other gentle folk of the kingdoms of Calontir, Meridies, Ansteorra, Outlands, and Middle, especially those of the Stronghold of Forgotten Sea, the Shire of Standing Stones, and the Barony of Three Rivers for their hospitality and generosity. I would like to thank Thomas Ezell for being my guide and contact for Civil War reenactors. He found brotherhood, friendship, and a most satisfying way to relieve stress. Dyson Nickle was a gracious and amazing host and guide to east Texas Civil War reenactors. I am grateful to the gentlemen and ladies who reenact the Civil War and Faires for their chivalry, hospitality, and generosity sharing their feelings, experiences, and photographs. I thank the many SCA and other reenactors who have become my friends and have kept me connected to the Known World over the past several years.

I thank Deborah Pearsall, my doctoral advisor, for her support and enthusiasm as the importance of reenactment groups became more apparent, as well as her patience and guidance through my doctorate and dissertation. I would also like to thank my dissertation committee for their support and contributions to the initial research: Robin Kennedy, Louanna Furbee, Kathryn Coe, and Gery Ryan. Each provided unique and invaluable support. Peter Gardner for long talks about sacred time, role reversal, and the importance of paracultures. Catherine Chmidling, Suan Rickabaugh, and Shanna Francis accompanied me on fieldwork and Catherine patiently read draft after draft as the manuscript matured. Thomas Ezell, and Michael Dietz spent many hours reviewing numerous drafts of this project. Patricia Robyn Ezell Webster, sister extraordinaire for reading endless drafts and sharing her talent for turning a phrase. Any errors in this manuscript are mine and despite their hard work. I thank my colleagues at Stephen F. Austin State University's Social and Cultural Analysis Department for their support and contributions through discussions and reviews on this text, especially: Ray Darville, Jeff Roth, Randi Barnes-Cox, J.B. Watson, Peggy Moss, and the always helpful Dianne Dentice. My thanks also to Catherine Chmidling, Natasha Grando, Michael Dietz, and Diane Ballinger for their reviews for the 2nd edition. My most sincere gratitude to the 3rd edition reviewers. Dianne Dentice for our collaboration on social movements and southern identity and for slogging through calf-deep water and mud in the field. J.B. Watson for his always optimistic support and commiseration as well as just the perfect nudges on theory and interpretation—thank you for Goffman and lessons on the Tyranny of the Shoulds. Catherine Chmidling for our collaborative work on the nature of reenacting.

Continuing my continuing research was made possible by the Office of Research and Sponsored Programs at Stephen F. Austin State University for funding additional research and fieldwork through a Research Enhancement Program Minigrant and a Travel Grant. Finally, I would like to thank the editors and staff at Kendall-Hunt for their patience and support in transforming a dissertation into a book. Special thanks to Stephanie Ramirez for getting this book started and Taylor Knuckey and Elizabeth Cray for coaxing this third edition and the new eBook and ancillaries from me.

This book is dedicated to Sasha and Robyn, who made their appearances in this world while I was writing and editing and have grown up into dedicated fangirls on their own thanks to me and their dad, my partner in fandom- Alex. Finally, but definitely not least: to my SFASU Anthropology students. You have made me constantly work to explain and present not just reenactors but anthropological theory and ethnography. I hope that this book is much the better for it.

PART I

Ethnography and Anthropology

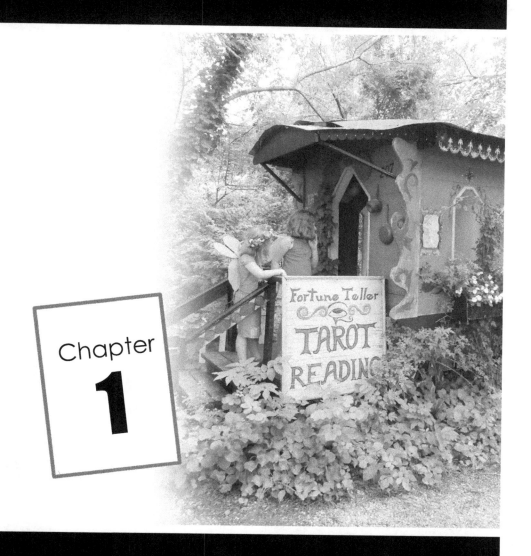

Chapter

1

Why Study Reenactors? Preconceptions and Biases

What Are Reenactors?

The topic of this book is the unique set of cultural practices found in reenactors. **Reenactors** are people who act out characters, behaviors, and events from a particular historic period, event, or fantasy genre. They are hobbyists, but the term *hobby* often fails to capture the amount of time, effort, and detail invested in many reenactors' re-creations. Much time is spent research-ing the time period to be enacted, especially the customs, clothing, accessories, grooming, and historical details. A reenactor works hard to construct a **period** (historically-accurate) **persona** or **impression**. (A **persona** is the character, role, or avatar being "played" or assumed by the reenactor. Different reenacting groups prefer different terms such as persona, impression, or more rarely, "character.") Try thinking of the persona/impression as the avatar you would choose to play in a video game. or the role or character you would play in a movie. Reenactors spend a great deal of time learning history and culture to create and develop their personae, which are often subject to peer review by other reenactors. **Impressions** are made up of a personality profile, behaviors, a background story in historical context, clothing, artifacts, accessories, and even grooming to construct as realistic a portrayal as possible.

Reenactors are different than people who merely wear a costume for an event like a party or an entertainment job. Unlike actors or the casual party-goer, reenactors do not wear costumes. Their **kit (impression kit)**–which includes the clothing, accessories, genre-specific artifacts, and even grooming–are designed to help them get into character. The kit helps the reenactor to get into character as a part of a special form of method acting in which they try to experi-ence the reality of the time period. Many historical reenactors do **living history** performances that are used to educate the public because of this authenticity. Whereas a person wearing a costume is aware that they are wearing something which is fake, the reenactor attempts to become the person who makes the costume real clothing. This is why many reenactors are often angered by comments about their "costumes", when they are, from their viewpoint, wearing their uniform, **garb**, finery, etc. . . Calling their painstaking recreation a costume accuses them of fakeness and often even jars them "out of the moment", ruining the experience of reenacting for them. Reenactors who are accustomed to living history performances, however, have learned to interpret such questions as genuine expressions of interest and incorporate them into their narrative and educational activities. Simply using a word other than "costume," such as "kit", "uniform", "garb", or just "clothing" shows recognition of their hard work and serves as a compliment to reenactors. It will also often elicit a stream of enthusiastic explanation of their persona and the research and effort they have invested in the details of their impression kit.

Reenactors are part of social groups that work together to recreate essential elements of a shared time period or genre. They create social structures and interact as a functional subculture with it's own norms, practices, and customs.

Reenacting Genres: Who, What, and When?

Reenactor groups are defined by what genre the members re-enact. **Historical reenactors** choose a specific time period, cultural setting, or set of events as their genre.

The time period chosen for reenactment is usually a matter of personal preference (an enthu-siasm for a particular time, culture, or event), convenience (what reenactment groups are accessible to the hobbyist), and cultural heritage. **Genre**, or **period**, are the most common terms for the time period, event, or style reenacted.

The most common historical reenactment genres in the United States are Civil War, Revolutionary War, European Medieval and Renaissance, and Rendezvous. As you can see, war- or military-based reenactment genres are very popular in the US as well as worldwide. Growing in popularity over the last several decades are other military reenactment periods such as World Wars I and II, Vietnam, and Korea. World Wars I and II, the Roman, Greek, and Viking periods, Bronze/Iron Age Celtic, and the Napoleonic Wars are very popular reenactment genres in Europe. In the U.S., Canada, Australia, and Scotland; Scottish Highland living history is very popular, especially by descendants of the Scots who either emigrated or were transported after the battle of Culloden. Colonial-type genres such as Rendezvous, which are very popular in the United States and Canada, with enthusiasts reenacting early colonial life, Lewis & Clark, the Old West, Cowboys, early settlers to the West, and Spanish Colonials. Rendezvous, in particular, is a popular genre in Canada, the Northern U.S., the Midwest, and the Smokey Mountains which focuses on fur trappers, explorers and mountain men from the 1750s–1840s in the Americas and is quite different from military-oriented reenacting from the same time period. In Texas, the Spanish-American War, the War of Texas Independence, the American Civil War, World War and Texas Republican reenactments are also popular. There are even Pirate reenactors in the Caribbean and along the southeastern U.S. coast.

Medieval and Renaissance reenacting includes both Renaissance Faires and groups like the Society for Creative Anachronism, which are quite different despite their shared time period. The Society for Creative Anachronism, started in Berkeley, California in 1966, has spread to Canada, United Kingdom, Sweden, Finland, Germany, Italy, Greece, Romania, Japan, New Zealand, South Africa, and Australia. The S.C.A. currently (as of 2017) has about 30,000 paying members, with many more people who participate in local events without joining the official organization, and is probably the single largest reenactment organization. In sheer numbers by genre, American Civil War reenactors are estimated to number anywhere from 40,000–60,000, but these are spread among many different individual organizations and difficult to count both because of their sheer number and the fact that many reenactors join more than one group. In this book, I focus on the genres with which I have had the most interaction and fieldwork the S.C.A., Renaissance Faire, and Civil War reenactors.

Fantasy Reenactors

Though this book focuses on historical reenactors, there are a great number of people who enjoy fantasy reenactment. **Fantasy reenactors** seek to enact non-historical realms or universes. Common fantasy genres for reenactment are those from comic books, anime, fantasy worlds, horror, science fiction, and RPGs (Role-Playing Games). Star Wars and Star Trek are particularly popular genres for reenactment, as are vampire-related fantasies. Anime culture and LARPs (Live Action Role Playing) of many genres are very popular. Because fantasy reenactments do not have the anchor of historic locations, they often occur in settings such as science fiction/ fantasy conventions, gaming sessions, and online environments. These fantasy reenactors are sometimes organized into coherent units or groups like historical reenactors, but are also very likely to be free agents. It is interesting to note that while many reenactors pick a single genre, be it historical or fantasy, some reenactors enjoy multiple genres of reenacting, depending on their mood. For Games-oriented fans, there are LARPs, mystery, spy, mafia, superhero, science fiction, and military action reenactment games. A large following exists for Lord of the Rings genre reenacting, especially in Australia and New Zealand. Some even retrace the locations of Peter Jackson's recent films in New Zealand.

It is important to note that Renaissance Faires and Festivals, while they are often historical reenactments, often include fantasy reenactors, too. While the Faires are centered around Renaissance-themed characters and events like Henry the Eighth, numerous cosplay and fantasy genres are also present at the Faire. Many Faires will have a mix of fantasy and historical themed events, merchants, shows, and activities.

Social Factors and Negative Misconceptions

Most people in the United States and Canada have heard of reenactors, particularly of Civil War reenactors and medieval European reenactors like the Society for Creative Anachronism (S.C.A.). To outsiders, these activities are often viewed as very marginal or "weird." When I mention that I've researched reenactors, people's responses range from neutral ["Why do they do that?"] to positive ["Wow, I'm glad someone is keeping the history alive"] to the negative ["Aren't those guys a little nuts?", "Why would anyone do that?", "Aren't they all racists?"] Context seems to be an important factor here: reenactors are a fun addition to museum events and heritage festivals, but they are often mocked if people encounter them in everyday life. Many **social factors** influence how people react to reenactors, such as 1) negative portrayal in popular culture or media, 2) regional history and affiliation to a particular side of a war, 3) one's ethnicity, political, or religious identity, and 4) American norms about acceptable role play and recreation. The media, in particular, portray reenactors as comical and outside the norm. Participation in historical or fantasy reenactment is an accepted trope in movies or television shows for "weird", "nerdy", and/or "crazy." Particular genres of reenactment are popular, respected, or ridiculed based upon local history. For example, Revolutionary War reenactment is very popular in the Eastern U.S. but almost unheard of in the West while Rendezvous is ubiquitous in the North and almost non-existent in the Southern U.S. Regionalism mingles with ethnicity and political affiliation in the example of Confederate Civil War reenactment–which is viewed very differently not only by geographic region but by social and ethnic affiliation. Religion makes fantasy reenactment associated with magic or supernatural creatures taboo in many rural areas of the U.S. Finally, social norms for participation in gaming, role play, and public ritual are important social factors that affect the social cost for people participating in reenacting role play. Other people have even more negative ideas about reenactors that should be addressed and dispelled in order to let the reader approach the subject with an open mind.

Nostalgia and White Supremacy

An important set of social factors that interact to cause negative views about reenactors are the regional political, historical, and ethnic contexts of how different people think about the American Civil War. A common misconception about American Civil War reenactors is that they are white supremacists, motivated by racism and nostalgia for white supremacy. In *"A Century of Civil War Observance,"* John Hope Franklin (1962) said that Civil War observances, from flags to parades to plaques, were "unworthy of the vaunted American goal of freedom and equality." His argument was that Negroes (the common term for African Americans or Afro-Caribbeans at that time) may no longer be slaves in legal terms, but were certainly not yet full and equal citizens with the rights and freedoms of other Americans. Because of this, Franklin held, the Civil War was a failure. He was particularly critical of early reenactments that were taking place in the centennial remembrance of the war.

> *"Sham battles are being staged to stimulate the imagination and to encourage viewers to second-guess the outcome." (pg 104)*
>
> *"Why is it that a mature, somewhat sophisticated, and indisputably powerful nation would subject itself to ridicule before the entire world with the vulgar reenactment of the Battle of Bull Run?" (pg 104)*

People who object to Civil War reenactment on the grounds of racism associate the Civil War simply with slavery and white supremacy. Many African Americans, in particular, are offended by what they see as glorification of the Confederacy and the Southern antebellum period which practiced slavery. To these individuals, the Confederate Battle Flag, Confederate uniforms, and remembrances of the Civil War seem like a celebration of white supremacy. This is reinforced when such symbols are proudly displayed and used by actual white supremacist groups such as the Ku Klux Klan. To be specific, people who object on these grounds object to portraying *Confederates* from the Civil War as anything but slaveholding villains. They are all right with movies or reenactments that portray Southerners as ideological caricatures of evil slaveholders but want no absolution for the sins of the Confederacy and no casual display of any symbols of the Confederacy, including the Battle Flag of the Virginia Guard (the "Stars and Bars" that was inaccurately popularized as "The" Confederate Flag in the 1960s as a part of centenniel celebrations and backlash to the Civil Rights Movement). In short, Southerners are the bad guys.

The image of General Sherman still reminds Southerners of the brutal Atlanta Campaign. Think of Margaret Mitchell's Gone With the Wind, *with the Antebellum Period portrayed as a fairy tale that represented the peak of Southern Culture, with Confederate officers nobly fighting for state's rights.* Copyright Jupiter Images.

In the deep South, by contrast, Union soldiers are often the boogeymen, appearing as ominous characters in local folklore. The early Klan are portrayed as Southern men protecting their own (especially white women) from occupying carpetbagger Yankees. Less extreme *southern identity* movements associates Confederate symbols with local pride and heritage versus oppression from Federal or Union oppression. The same feelings are why Confederate flags are often displayed by Libertarians, the Tea Party, and anti-government groups. (Dentice and Chandler-Ezell 2008)

The problem with this is that it ignores that the Civil War was about much more than slavery. Franklin himself explains that he is upset not that the Civil War was being remembered, but that it was memorialized in an overly simplistic way that ignores its true significance. He holds that the Civil War was the unifying national experience of the United States and should be remembered in that way. His point is that the Civil War and Reconstruction experience was the furnace that forged a new, unified United States and Americans with a shared national identity, regardless of which side of the war our ancestors chose. Because of it's salience to our cultural identity, it is natural that we would have a great interest in this conflict and time period. Civil War reenactment groups are focused on this goal. They seek to experience this time when our national character was forged and then communicate that to their audience. Their research is both a personal quest to discover what it was like to actually be in the shoes of the people they are memorializing and to make sure that the lessons learned in the War Between the States are never forgotten. In anthropological terms, they seek to gain an insider's, or "emic" perception, through participant observation.

In their own words:

> "The Nineteenth Century Living History Association and its subsidiaries are volunteer organizations dedicated to the serious research, study, preservation, and accurate description of persons and events of the American Civil War, both Union and Confederate. Furthermore, the various Corporations and its Board of Directors denounces racism, racial supremacists, hate groups and other groups or individuals that misuse or desecrate the symbols of the United States of America and/or the former Confederate States of America; and has no modern political agenda or status." http://www.texas-brigade.com/frmain.htm

Most of these groups also require that members be willing to portray either Union or Confederate soldiers as needed to make the most realistic reenactments. Some travel to events with the paraphernalia for two alternate impressions just in case.

The greatest argument against inherent racism in Civil War reenactment is the popularity of African American reenactors. While the popular film *Glory* brought attention to the African American soldiers who fought for the Union, a more recent documentary by Stan Armstrong is *Black Confederates: The Forgotten Men in Gray*. African Americans participate in Civil War reenacting, portraying people from both the Confederate and Union sides.

Yet another consideration is the cultural importance of the Antebellum period, the Civil War, and Reconstruction for Southerners. In the South, Civil War reenactors are viewed as stewards of Southern culture and spark a personal nativistic connection in people who feel personally connected to the Civil War. Many southerners know Civil War stories of their great-grandparents and other relatives. Civil War historic sites and artifacts of the Antebellum period saturate the Southern landscape. The Antebellum period serves as the dawn of civilization for the South. It is viewed nostalgically as a fairy tale time, romanticized as the peak of culture and beauty for many, particularly as it is portrayed in novels, movies, and other media. It has become it's own mythololology and its symbols are a part of the implicit religion of regional identity for Southern American identity. In contrast to this, the destruction from the war and Reconstruction were times of hardship and poverty which the South endured much more than the North. The Southerners were the only Americans who've ever been invaded, conquered, and occupied on their home soil. (Though the Native Americans experienced this, they were viewed as "Other", even subhuman, by European-descent colonists.) In the South, Americans battled

Brothers in arms wearily return to camp after a long day reenacting the Battle of Shiloh in Tennessee. Contrary to popular misconceptions, not all reenactors are Caucasian, and many play roles on both sides as needed.
Photo by Steve Shore

their own people, even their own families.) The horrors of the war and the long decades of poverty which followed made the Antebellum period seem even more romantic by contrast. The Civil War provided regional legends and folklore from the dawn of Southern culture. The signs and symbols of the war, especially the Confederacy, are associated with the great deeds of ancestors for many Southerners, and it is difficult for many to forget this even when they know those same symbols are painful to others. As a result, while others may have negative perceptions of Civil War reenactments, they are often very positively viewed by Southerners. As a result, Civil War-related symbols are often appropriated by **Southern identity movements.** (Dentice 2008, 2009) Are there people who appropriate the symbols and mythology of the Confederacy as part of a racist agenda? Yes. There are even people who play at the Civil War as a caricature of white supremacy and domination. This is not the goal or attitude of most reenactors, however, and most Civil War reenactors shun the racists who try to pollute their community.

At the writing of the first edition of this book, the flag of the Confederacy was still flown in many former Confederate States (including as one of the Nine Flags in Nacogdoches and Six Flags of Texas). The flag has been taken down from daily use in many of those states in the midst of much controversy. As of early 2017, monuments and statues of Confederate soldiers are being removed from many cities across the south, calling into question how we, as a society, relate to the Civil War 150 years later. This sort of culture clash will continue as long as characters from the war are simplistically viewed as good guys and bad guys in particular regions. The goal of living history is to actually breathe life and complexity into these characters by portraying them in a realistic way. By portraying "real" people with complex motivations and personal histories, reenactors do much to dispel simplistic stereotypes of the people who lived through the Civil War. Their fantasies and playacting are done to teach a more realistic perspective on the war. It is serious play and the historical focus combines with method acting to create more personal experiences of heritage and historical perspective.

"Get a Life" and "Grow Up"

A fourth major social factor that leads to negative perceptions of reenactors is related to cultural norms in the U.S. As a society, we have far less public ritual and role play than many other cultures. We also have less adult play. Other reenactors are often accused of immaturity, or a failure to differentiate reality from fantasy. While there have been reenactors that were psychologically unwell, they are rare, and this is simply not true for most reenactors. There are **two major reasons** for the belief that reenactors are unable to discern fantasy from reality.

First, the assumption is that if reenactors are "just playing", then they must be immature. Playing dress-up and wearing costumes is seen as a childish activity in our society. It is neither productive nor normal adult behavior, so it is frivolous.

Anthropologically speaking, this is simply untrue. Numerous ritual behaviors in modern society involve stereotypical behaviors and costumes to "act out" symbolic rites. Festivities associated with holidays (Christmas, Halloween, Easter etc.) festivals (Mardi Gras, Homecoming events, prom), and rites of passage (weddings graduation confirmations) use ritualized role play.

Many of the crafts and skills that reenactors learn take a great deal of practice and research, yet they are often viewed as esoteric or outdated. While some outsiders are excited and enjoy seeing that someone is preserving knowledge of older times, investing so much time and often money in a craft that is today carried out much more quickly by machines is often viewed as extravagant. The very lack of efficiency and the imprecision characteristic of handmade items or older technology is prized by reenactors and living historians for its uniqueness. Even a crookedly stitched costume is proudly displayed to other reenactors as a product of their own hands. It is well received as a sign of the willingness to learn and try despite setbacks by other reenactors. Stories about the mistakes and difficulties one has learning an old craft, especially the creation of garments, is a common topic of friendly chatting and socializing among reenactors. Eventual mastery of these skills gains the reenactor prestige and higher social status amongst his peers. Classes, workshops, and study groups on older skills, crafts, and knowledge make up a large portion of reenactor interactions and activities. Social sharing of knowledge, experience, and materials is a method of bonding and integrating people into the reenacting community. A new recruit's first activity with the group is working with other reenactors to learn how to create the material artifacts (especially clothing) needed to portray their new alternate persona. As they help mentor the new recruit in material culture, the more experienced members of the community also establish friendships and pass on the social aspects of their culture. Developing an impression kit or a new persona is part of formal enculturation into reenacting society.

Second, if outsiders accept that reenactors are playing seriously, they then assume that it is a sign of aberrant psychology. Most of the scholarly writings on reenactors make a point of diagnosing reenactors with Fantasy-Prone personalities and even personality disorders or defects. Their conclusions assume that mature, psychologically healthy individuals do not play act. This ignores the ubiquity of ritual role-playing in human culture. Anthropological research shows the importance of rituals and role-playing. *Rituals are basic cultural mechanisms for communicating identity, ideology, and camaraderie as well as for acting out significant cultural events.* Victor Turner's research (1964) into the function of rituals shows the importance role-playing for alleviating stress, forming social bonds, and experiencing **communitas**. This will be discussed in greater detail as we learn more about the different types of reenactors in chapters 5–7.

Weird Is Beautiful to the Social Scientist

The very wealth of misconceptions about reenacting makes it an interesting anthropological topic. The general goal of people within a society is to be viewed as **culturally competent.** This means knowing the social rules and norms and being able to successfully fill accepted social roles. People who do not manage to maintain a socially acceptable role frequently suffer anxiety and social stigma in addition to endangering their status and success. They are considered to be **marginalized**—on the edges of society.

Anthropologists and other social scientists study marginalized people or groups of people for a variety of reasons. Common research questions about marginalized groups include trying to understand why a group becomes marginalized; how their social status affects their mental and physical health; how to improve their access to educational, economic, and health resources; and what their social dynamics are.

Whether it is viewed positively or negatively by outsiders, reenacting is definitely viewed as doing something that is outside the norm. Marginalizing yourself by doing something that makes you noticeably *deviant* (outside normal range of behavior disregard) is socially risky and may negatively affect your social status. Participating in reenacting is merely socially dangerous—there are usually no serious risks of being physically harmed in modern Western culture, but it is noticeably outside the norm and causes people to react and view the reenactor as deviant. Why, then, do people take this social risk?

SCA fighters battle for the Crown, Crown Lists Tourney in the SCA Kingdom of Calontie, 2001
Photo by Karol Chandler-Ezell

That is what this book hopes to answer. The simplest answer is that reenacting fills a social and psychological need. The experience of reenacting and the social atmosphere of being part of the reenactment community gives participants something that they do not get out of their everyday, mainstream lives. The following chapters seek to demonstrate how those needs are filled.

The second chapter describes the ethnographic method in cultural anthropology and introduces ideas from studying culture, while methods of fieldwork are introduced in Chapter 3. As stated in the Preface, I take a cultural and adaptive approach to this study, asking "why do people participate in reenacting?" and "what function does it serve?" By using sociocultural theories of culture change and adaptive behavior, we can begin to understand the important and adaptive role that reenactment participation plays for individuals. The fieldwork is discussed in Chapters 3 and 4. In the following chapters, the Society for Creative Anachronism, Renaissance Faire, Civil War, and other reenactment groups are described and discussed. Revitalization Movements and Invention of Tradition, two important sociocultural theories which apply to nostalgic culture processes, are discussed. A comparative approach is used to point out both the similarities and differences in the groups. Finally, we return to the questions of how sociocultural theory sheds new light on much of the reenactment phenomenon in Chapter 8.

Name _____ Date _____

I. Basic information about reenactors:

1. What is a **reenactor**?

_____

_____

_____

2. ... and what is a **reenactor** *not?*

_____

_____

_____

3. What are some popular genres chosen by reenactors? List at least 4, giving the name of the **period**.

1. _____

2. _____

3. _____

4. _____

4. How does a **historical reenactor** differ from a **fantasy reenactor**? Define each.

_____

_____

_____

5. What are some common *negative* beliefs people have about reenactors?

_____

_____

_____

6. What evidence supports or fails to support these negative impressions? Given this evidence, do these negative impressions have merit? Explain.

_____

_____

_____

7. What are some *positive* reactions people have to reenactors?

_____

_____

_____

8. What 4 social factors contribute to positive reactions to certain types of reenactors versus negative ones?

_____

_____

_____

_____

9. What types of reenactment genres do you expect to develop in future years? Explain.

_____

_____

_____

10. After reading Chapter 1, what fact about reenactors was most surprising to you? Describe and why? _____

_____

_____

_____

Name _____ Date _____

II. Ethnographic Practice Activities: Surveying common perceptions of Reenactors:

Assignment A

1. List the types of reenactors you had heard about before this book in the table below.

2. After making your list, go back and rate your impression of each type of reenactor as positive (+) or negative (−). Then, describe your initial impressions of each type of reenactor. Finally, use the last column on the right to mark whether your opinion was changed positively (+) or negatively (−) by reading Chapter 1.

List types of Reenactors	Initial Impression? + | −	Describe your initial impressions of each type of reenactor	Opinion changed? + | −

Name _____ Date _____

Assignment B

    3. Now go and survey a friend or family member. (You may need to interview a few people to find someone who has heard of reenactors.) Ask them to list any types of reenactors they know about. Ask them their impressions of each type. Then ask them if they've actually seen any of those reenactors.

List types of Reenactors	Initial Impression? + | −	Describe your initial impressions of each type of reenactor	Have you ever seen this type of reenactors? Where?

4. **Follow-up questions to your survey:** Now that you have a small set of data surveying your own knowledge and that of a friend, compare the information.

a. Compare your list to the one you gathered from your friends. How do they differ?

_____

_____

_____

b. How would you describe the way you and the people you surveyed view reenactors?

_____

_____

_____

c. Think about social factors discussed in Chapter 1. How might opinions about reenactors vary in other states or regions of the country based upon how those social factors influence opinions?

_____

_____

_____

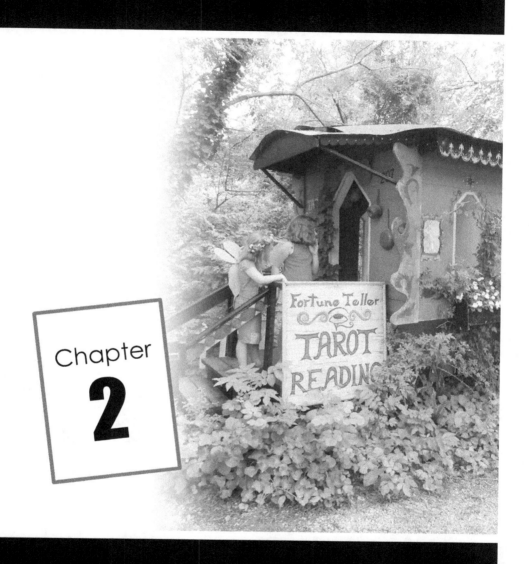

Chapter 2

Ethnographic Studies and Anthropology

Ethnographic Studies: How Anthropologists Study Living People

The study of culture is the basis of cultural anthropology, also known as ethnology. The root *"ethnos"* comes the Greek for "people", and is used to refer to a culture. Ethnology, then, is the study of people, particularly what makes them "a people", or society–their culture. Many other disciplines study people, but both the approach and methods used in anthropology set it apart from other fields of study focused on humans and their activities.

The anthropological approach is *holistic,* seeking to integrate multiple aspects of the human experience, including the biology, history, psychology, and social and physical environments. The anthropological approach is four-field, combining multiple lines of evidence and diverse perspectives on a problem. Unlike many other scientific or humanistic fields, anthropological research is conducted through fieldwork, or gathering data from a naturalistic setting instead of a laboratory. People are studied in their natural social and physical environments, not in a laboratory or as a part of a contrived experiment. The observations are usually directly performed by the anthropologist instead of by proxy through surveys. This separates it from many other disciplines that study humans and their behavior, such as psychology and some sociological studies.

The methods anthropologists use in studying people include cross-cultural comparisons and the ethnographic method. An **ethnography** is a writing about a people or culture from an anthropological perspective. It is the product of an ethnographic study. Doing ethnographic fieldwork is the process of discovering, studying, and describing a people as you are among them. Part of the professional training of a cultural anthropologist is learning to conduct ethnographic fieldwork.

Ethnographic methods for fieldwork include observation, especially participant observation, interviews, life histories, surveys, censuses, taxonomies, language catalogs, and kinship studies. Ethnographic methods used in this project are discussed in greater detail in Chapters 3 and 4. The anthropologist takes on the role of a student or sometimes even a child as they learn what it means to be a member of a society. In the early days of anthropology, young ethnographers were sent to study "their people", usually a fairly small group of non-Western, non-Industrial people who were considered "primitives" by white Westerners of the past. Today anthropologists study groups of various sizes and are increasingly studying complex societies around the world. While anthropologists still study people in remote areas or in small-scale societies, they also study industrial populations, too. One's fieldwork site could be in the jungle or the arctic, but it could also be in a hospital, at a fair, stadium, or space station.

Ethnographic field work in anthropology is guided by theory. Theoretical concepts guide the formation of research questions and the data to be gathered. This chapter presents theoretical concepts relevant to the study of reenactors and paracultures.

Subcultures, Microcultures, and Paracultures: Studying Complex Societies

As someone who takes an adaptive approach, I am interested in investigating counter-culture movements and subculture patterns. In particular, I am interested in how people cope with stressors from their environment, health, and culture's pressures. To do this, and to understand how anthropologists study complex societies, it is useful to know how to classify and organize the different levels of society and groupings within a larger, complex society. To begin, cultures can be divided up into subcultures. **Subcultures** are groupings of people within a larger culture that define coherent, separate groups of individuals sharing a culture: i.e. history, language, religion, identifiable badges, and practices. Examples of subcultures include Hmong immigrant communities in Canada or Cajuns in Louisiana. While subcultures exist at many levels, they are coherent systems, classified hierarchically as a smaller unit within a larger culture. So regional variations of a culture like being "Southern" in the U.S. as well as being a "Down-Easter," "Texan," or Appalachian would also be a subcultural category. Members of subcultures are fully integrated into that culture either by enculturation from childhood or by the process of joining the group.

Anthropologists working in complex societies also focus on even smaller divisions of cultures. In very large societies, even subcultures may be very large, with a large and diverse membership that would be difficult to fully understand in a holistic and complete ethnographic study. One way to make smaller studies more feasible is to work with microcultures. **Microcultures** are smaller social categories with specialized knowledge and customs. They differ from subcultures in that they

Renaissance garb appropriate for an impression. Note period-appropriate jewelry, hairstyle, and mannerisms. Proper curtseying is essential to a medieval or renaissance lady, SCA or Ren Faire.
Copyright Jupiter Images.

do not define a whole way of life (McCurdy et al. 2005). Microcultures tend to be associated with one aspect of members' lives, such as their occupation, recreational groups, and other activities. People within a microculture share a set of behaviors, specialized language, and knowledge. Some typical examples of microcultures include firefighters, college sororities or fraternities, sports teams, surfers, and many more groups you encounter daily. Microcultures are useful for understanding slices of a larger culture, especially particular contexts of daily life.

For my fieldwork, I was studying historical and fantasy reenactors. Despite their similarities to microcultures and subcultures, historical and fantasy reenactors differed in several qualitative ways. Reenactor cultural groups are not as large as subcultures, and reenactors are still members of different and larger subcultures. Reenactor culture is not just a microculture either, because the transitions between participating in mainstream culture and participating in reenacting culture as an alternate persona exist in parallel. People transition between the two, but keep them as separate identities within themselves, choosing which is the outward social identity at different times.

When actively performing a reenactment, the everyday self is submerged and replaced by the alternate persona and culture. If participants in alternative cultural groupings like reenactment groups are actually moving periodically back and forth into this parallel culture instead of converting fully to members of stable full-time subcultures, they are better described as being part of a *paraculture*. *Para-* in this usage refers to the paraculture being both parallel and outside or in tandem to everyday culture. Paracultures are tightly knit groups such as historical reenacting which make their hobbies intense, shared "cultures" that saturate much of their daily life and self-identity while operating parallel to mainstream life. Members of paracultures are distinct in that they "slip into" an alternate role from the paraculture.

This role-play and switching the level of social interaction has precedent in other culltural phenomena. Cross-cultural studies show that the practice of temporarily taking on alternate social roles is a common practice in many societies and allows social freedom to perform rituals, escape social pressure, and mitigate stressful situations. **Rituals** are symbolic stereotyped and often repetitive behaviors that 1) serve as a focus and 2) communicate symbolically. I argue that members

SCA reenactors study details from texts, tapestries, and stained glass art to create authentic reproductions.
Copyright Jupiter Images.

of paracultures take on alternate personas as a way of coping with psychological and cultural stress, and that it is an adaptive behavior designed to meet people's underlying needs, fears, and even perceived threats to their health and well-being. Reenacting rituals, then, function like rituals common to other cultures, with role play as a way to interact with others and share the experience in a creative way.

Studying paracultures allows us not only to learn the specialized practices of a cultural grouping but also can provide insight to the stresses from the larger culture with which people are trying to cope. In the new two chapters, we learn about ethnographic methods which are useful for studying cultures, subcultures, microcultures, and paracultures.

Name _____ Date _____

I. Learning More About Ethnography

Assignment A: Reading Ethnographies

Choose an ethnography (you can choose one from the list on the next page or another, as instructed by your professor.) Read the ethnography and write a summary, taking care to note the following things:

1. Author's name and training.

2. When did the fieldwork take place?

3. Who, what cultural group was portrayed in the ethnography?

4. Was this a culture? A subculture? A microculture? Explain how you determined this.

5. Where in the world is the group studied?

6. Describe the culture briefly in terms of their economy, subsistence strategy, political system, religious system, marriage patterns, and other cultural structures as described by the ethnographer.

Your instructor may have you complete a second part of this assignment after you complete Chapters 3 and 4 of this book.

To Learn More, Try One or More of These Ethnographies:

Benedict, Ruth. 1946. The Chrysanthemum and the Sword: Patterns of Japanese Culture.

Chagnon, Napoleon. 1984. Yanoamo: The Fierce People. (Case Studies in Anthropology) Wadsworth Publishing.

Evans-Pritchard, E. E. 1937. Witchcraft, Oracles, and Magic among the Azande.

Fernea, Elizabeth Warnock. 1969. Guests of the Sheik: An Ethnography of an Iraqi Village. Doubleday.

Mead, Margaret. 1928. Coming of Age in Samoa: A Psychological Study of Primitive Youth for Western Civilisation.

Malinowski, Bronislaw. 1922. Argonauts of the Western Pacific.

Mooney, James. 1900. Myths of the Cherokee.

Mooney, James. 1965. The Ghost Dance Religion and the Sioux Outbreak of 1890. University of Chicago Press.

Quinlan, Marsha B. 2003. From the Bush: The Front Line of Healthcare in a Caribbean Village. (Case Studies in Anthropology) Wadsworth Publishing.

Rappaport, Roy A. 1984. Pigs for the Ancestors: Ritual in the Ecology of a New Guinea People. Yale University Press.

Turnbull, Colin M. 1988. Forest People. Peter Smith Publisher.

I. Learning More About Ethnography:

Assignment B: Advanced Searches of Ethnographic Databases

The Human Relations Area Files (HRAF) is a massive database of ethnographic information from around the world. First compiled and organized by George Peter Murdock in 1937 on library-style index cards, the HRAF is now a massive electronic database available on the Internet at http://www.yale.edu/hraf.htm. If your university has a subscription to access the database, you can search through more than 800,000 pages of text and images from more than 365 cultural groups around the world. For those without university access to the database, you can learn much by using the public information available on the HRAF Web site.

With full HRAF access either online or through a copy at your university library, you can search the database for a variety of cultural elements and patterns, including the revitalization movements and cargo cults discussed in the latter parts of this book.

Information Search 1: Exploring and Learning to Use the HRAF

Review the material on the HRAF Web site and answer the following questions.

1. Why were the HRAF created?

_____

_____

_____

2. What sorts of documents were used to compile the HRAF?

_____

_____

_____

3. What is an OWC code?

_____

_____

_____

List some of them and what they mean.

_____

_____

_____

4. How are the cultures organized? Describe the levels of classification.

_____

_____

5. What is the OCM? How is it used?

_____

_____

_____

6. How are the OWC and OCM codes useful when you are using the database?

_____

_____

_____

Information Search 2: Finding Information on the HRAF Database

Part A

1. Your instructor will assign you a culture. Write it down here _____.

2. Find your culture's OWC code and write it here _____.

3. Go to the complete collections list and record what documents are available from that culture. Record the following information:

    a. The number of documents in the database _____

    b. The number of pages of text available _____

    c. The time period these documents cover _____

4. Print out the search results list and turn it in.

Now that you have searched by a culture, you are ready to try searching by other criteria. For instance, you could search by marriage type, kinship systems, or political systems. Look in the OCM Subjects/Codes list and pick a subject of interest to you.

Part B

Write your subject code here: _____

Now, run it as a search term and record the following information:

1. The number of documents in the database _____

2. How many cultures did you find under this search term? _____

3. Pick one record and summarize what information it contains on this topic.

Now that you know how to find information on the HRAF about a specific culture, you will be ready to complete information searches in the future.

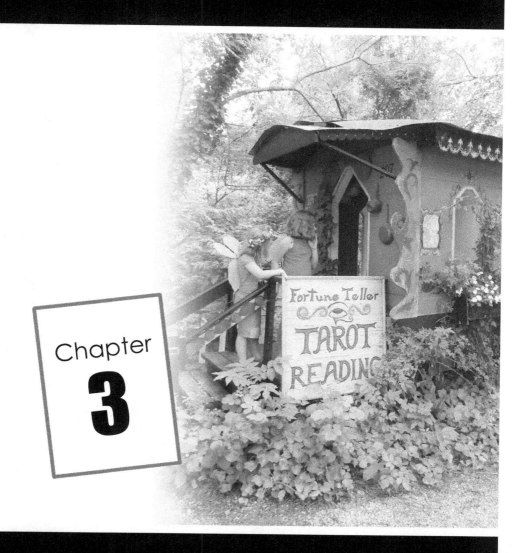

Chapter 3

Fieldwork Methods and Tools for Ethnographic Research

Methods and Fieldwork in Ethnography

How does one go about studying cultures, subcultures, and even smaller groups? The goals are to understand the point of view of the members of the society you are studying (the ***emic point of view***) and then to communicate that comprehension while gaining a scientific understanding and data that allows cross-cultural comparison and measurement of cultural phenomena (the ***etic point of view***). The researcher usually has specific questions to answer and/or hypotheses to test with the data they gather. The fieldwork methods chosen determine what kind of data the researcher can collect.

One of the most important steps in ethnographic fieldwork is research design. Clearly stating your research question and what data you need to answer those questions reveals what data collection methods you should use in the field if you want to be successful. What methods will work in your field site? How will it need to be analyzed? At every step, choice of method shapes the structure of the data gathered and its ultimate usefulness in understanding the anthropological phenomenon being investigated.

It is important, then, to choose the sampling techniques that are the best suited to answering the goals and questions of the project. Even more important is the precaution of ensuring that you, as the researcher, are actually gathering the appropriate units of data to actually answer your questions. Failure to gather the appropriate units results in a project with data that doesn't apply to your research questions and much frustration as you search for a way to "get at" the answers to your questions.

For most research questions, a variety of techniques can successfully gather similar forms of the same units of data, giving you some freedom to choose among methods. It is important to consider more than your own convenience as a researcher when choosing, though. Some techniques of data collection provide the bits of data in more desirable formats for the researcher, but they may be unpalatable (i.e. *boring*) to the consultants performing the task. The final methodology, then, must be a reasonable compromise between the researcher's desire for explicit, complete information in an easily-processed format and the consultants' patience for often tedious tasks.

This chapter describes several methods of gathering and analyzing data that can be used in a variety of settings. It is by no means a complete descriptive of all the data collection methods available in ethnography, but it is a simple introduction for beginning students. Once you master these basic skills, you can choose to apply them in topics of interest to you. At the end of this chapter are several small exercises which will give you practice with these new skills.

Basic Ethnographic Methods

Ethnography is a holistic, recorded description of a culture, subculture, or paraculture. Classically, an ethnography has been a *written* account, but the availability of visual and audio media has resulted in a growing number of multimedia ethnographies now that integrate sound and images. Doing ethnography is the process of collecting the information, or data, which will be used to describe and represent the people of a culture. A variety of methods are used in ethnography.

Most ethnographic projects, much like other scholarly work, begin with a **literature review** and **background research**. It's one of the reasons that science is so effective as a way of increasing knowledge: scientists build on what has gone before, increasing and refining what we know.

Much information about the culture being studied can be gathered from literature and document review. Many would-be ethnographers begin by trying to discover what, if anything, has already been recorded about the group or phenomena they wish to study. This preliminary background research can be quite invaluable. Imagine traveling to a remote location and setting up camp with a people, struggling to learn their language enough to even greet them properly, and spending a year in the field with them. . . . only to come back and discover that a complete dictionary of their language was available in your university library! Background research lets the researcher discover what has already been done (and what needs to be done) and make more informed and considered decisions about their research topic and questions. Another important, preliminary step in research is to conduct a small **pilot study**. A pilot study is a much smaller-scale project used to test the methods, tools, and/or field site. It lets you test how effective your strategies are before you commit to your longterm project. Several small pilots are sometimes used to test interview questions, equipment, and the feasibility of your research design. You get preliminary data and valuable insight into how to revise and improve your research questions and fieldwork plans from pilot studies. These research questions shape the rest of the project, determining who and where will be studied and what data needs to be collected. In the course of fieldwork, research questions are often refined and revised as new data is incorporated into the researcher's model, but the initial research questions are necessary for scientific inquiry.

Research Questions

Your **research question** is based upon what you want to learn. For instance, is your question "what rituals do the Cherokee observe throughout the life cycle?" If it was, then your research approach would need to include methods that would collect data about the Cherokee culture's idea of the life cycle and rites of passage. Quite simply, your research questions guide your research because they help you plan and decide what fieldwork you need to do. When your fieldwork is done, your data analysis and the report of your fieldwork presents your questions and the data you have collected to answer those questions.

Observation

Once a culture and preliminary research questions are selected, the first and most basic method in ethnographic fieldwork is to observe the culture in question. In the past, observation was a spectator sport, with outsiders recording the behaviors and characteristics of the people being observed much as ethologists did with animal behavior studies. This is part of the *etic*, or outsider's approach. The hallmark method of anthropological ethnography, however, is *participant observation*. In participant observation, the ethnographer participates in the activities being studied. By doing what the people being observed do, the ethnographer learns what it is like from the *emic*, or *insider's* perspective. Participant observation also greatly aids in establishing **rapport**, a feeling of closeness and empathy. The people are better able to relate to the ethnographer and can interact comfortably with the participant observer, often under the guise of helping them learn how to perform various activities properly. The ethnographer becomes much like a child being enculturated into the society, and members of the society are more at ease if they know where the ethnographer fits into the scheme of things. This can also be beneficial for the ethnographer in other ways. In this childlike learning role, mistakes that are offensive in adults are often laughed away as the mistakes of a child, and unintentional gaffs are more likely to be treated with tolerance and gently corrected. Often, key informants or elders in the society will take the ethnographer under their wing as a fictive child, providing them with a place in the society, much-appreciated social support, and entrée into aspects of cultural life that are not usually accessible to true outsiders. This closeness and incorporation into the society helps the ethnographer to enculturate and better understand the *emic perspective*.

What does the ethnographer observe? Descriptions of the culture include lists of the artifacts and behaviors observed. It is common to inventory the items for sale at different vendors, descriptions of homes, clothing, makeup, hairstyles, foods, currency, calendars, and customs. Often, photographs or video are recorded. Sample artifacts may be collected or purchased as examples. The observer should try to describe the social environment in as much detail as possible. Behaviors, in particular, should be carefully recorded.

Interviews

In the course of participant observation, the ethnographer collects data in many informal or loosely structured ways. Conversations overheard, casual commentary, and observations are all important sources of information. **Informal interviews** are conversations that the ethnographer has with consultants without a prestructured set of questions. A **formal interview** is usually planned and scheduled in a more formal setting and includes a preset list of questions to be asked by the ethnographer. The questions in the formal interview may be *structured* or *unstructured*, and the type of information requested may be either *qualitative* or *quantitative*. Most interviews include a little of each type of questions and data. *Structured questions* are those that require a bounded, or limited range of options for the answer. Survey questions and multiple choice exam questions are good examples of structured questions. For example, in a multiple choice exam question, there are usually two-five choices for the person to choose among, and all of the possible answers are there, provided by the questionnaire. An unstructured question is more like a short answer or essay question. The respondent is expected to answer in their own words or phrases and the answers may be totally unexpected or unanticipated by the interviewer. Either of these can be **quantitative**, that is, an answer that expresses a discrete quantity, or number. Quantitative data is naturally numeric, while Qualitative data is not naturally expressed in numbers. A **qualitative** question is not answered by a discrete quantity. Instead, it is an answer that provides a quality (blue, good, cold, sad, hate, etc . . .).

All of these have their place in describing a culture, and most ethnographies contain both qualitative and quantitative data. Over the course of an ethnography, a researcher usually uses both quantitative and qualitative questions. Qualitative unstructured questions are usually used for gathering exploratory data and learning enough background to prepare more informed structured questions. Ethnographers often collect life histories, personal narratives, and the answers to open-ended questions like "tell me about. . . ." or "why do people believe/do. . . . "

A summary or report of the information collected through these sorts of interviews are interpreted and presented by the ethnographer. Often, quotes from specific individuals are presented as representative of cultural beliefs. Analysis methods called **text analysis** are used to identify common **themes** or motifs and present them in a more systematic way than simply printing the complete text of all of the interviews. Themes often indicate the presence of cultural domains that the ethnographer studies in more detail.

Consultants vs. Informants

While individuals interviewed by ethnographers have traditionally been called informants, there are problems with this term. While the term *inform* may be defined as to "notify, apprise, enlighten, and advise," and is generally used in this way in the anthropological context, it is also used to mean to "accuse" and, "incriminate" (Abate 1997:pg 406). The term *informant* is defined in the Oxford Desk Dictionary and Thesaurus (Abate 1997) as one who "informs against or on" and is synonymous with the terms "stool pigeon" and "tattletale." The negative associations with the term informant have led many anthropologists to choose alternative terms with less negative associations (Bernard 1995). *Consultants* is a more modern standard term in anthropological ethnography now. *Subject* was commonly used in many social science studies and is still found in many medical studies, but it has almost as many negative and dehumanizing connotations as informant. Anthropology, Sociology, and Psychology often use the terms participant and respondent in place of the older terms informant and subject as a way of being respectful of the people they research. When speaking with my sample populations, I referred to them as "**consultants**", a term with more positive connotations. The term consultant is also used within the body of this text, as it is particularly appropriate to the people I interviewed. They were experts giving me specialized information and insight into reenactors, alternative culture, and herbalism.

Cultural Domains

A basic way to begin an ethnographic description and understanding of a group is to learn items of cultural knowledge like their special terms, artifacts, and customs. Collecting lists of the items in a cultural *domain,* or cognitive subject category, from several consultants lets a researcher describe the items included within those domains as well as variation among differing subgroups of my sampled consultants. For this to work, comparable bits of data, or units, are needed within each domain. There are several techniques for collecting systematic, comparable data on cultural domains. The most common techniques include free listing, pile sorting, triads, paired comparisons, and frame substitutions. I begin by discussing how the techniques relate to each other, then describe the characteristics and methods of free listing, pile sorting, and frame substitution. Once you know what data you need to collect, you can choose which technique is best for your ethnographic project.

Experts and Nonexperts

Who do you interview? An important pair of terms utilized in cultural research is "Expert" and "Nonexpert". These terms are commonly used in domain analysis to separate sampled populations into two, comparable categories. **Experts** are those that have extensive knowledge of a *domain* (area of knowledge) and are recognizable by their training, credentials, or even their ability to extensively and authoritatively use knowledge from that domain. Experts, quite simply, know more about a particular type of knowledge than nonexperts. **Nonexperts** have a general, or common level of knowledge about the topic, but very little or no specialized or advanced knowledge about the domain. These categories are highly useful for methods that measure differences in domain free list content and length as well as relational organization of items within domains by analysis of interview tasks such as free lists, pile sorts, triadic comparisons, frame substitutions sets, rankings, ratings and paired comparisons (Bernard 1995, Boster 1986 and 1994, Borgatti 1996). In general, experts will know more about an area of knowledge and be able to manipulate or talk about those bits of knowledge. For example, a botanical expert will know many more types of plants and be able to name, describe, identify, and organize information about those plants than someone who is not an expert in botany. A nonexpert in botany may know a few types of plants by common name, and maybe a few life forms (tree, grass, bush..) and genera (oak, palm, pine tree), but not be able to name as many as an expert or to competently organize the information.

If a researcher has experts and nonexperts complete the same interview tasks, experts will usually supply much more knowledge in greater detail than nonexperts. Why not just interview experts then? Well, in some cases, this is what the researchers do. A relatively small sample of experts will give you extensive knowledge about a domain. Each interview will take a great deal of time, but you can gather a great deal of detailed, accurate, and expertly arranged information. The problem is that most people in a society are nonexperts in most domains. So, to understand common knowledge and get a good, emic understanding of how most people in the society understand a domain, you need to interview nonexperts may provide the information in a much different way that is still important to the bulk of the population of a cultural group, since there are far more nonexperts than experts in most populations.

The analysis of data comparing experts and nonexperts is used to describe the *intracultural variation* in cognitive knowledge, beliefs, and structuring for a particular domain. Usually, the required characteristics for classification of consultants as either experts and nonexperts are defined in literature review or exploratory fieldwork prior to either the experimental fieldwork or interview analysis. If a researcher is uncertain of how to identify experts, there are methods for identifying experts and nonexperts within a sample population when they are unknown, by looking at their responses to freelists or other interview questions. Experts know more bits, or units of information (the particle model of knowledge); and they know more about how to organize and explain all the bits of information they know (the wae model of knowledge.) Analyzing your interview data from the cultural domain you are studying to look for these patterns is a part of **Cultural Consensus Modeling**. CCM evaluates the expertise of your consultants by how many "particles" or "items" of knowledge they list as well as how well they agree with the rest of the sample group. (Romney et al. 1986, 1987, D'Andrade 1987). Alternately, the "wave" approach to identifying experts vs. nonexperts evaluates not only how many pieces of knowledge consultants have, but more importantly, how *deep* their knowledge of the domain is in terms of functional ability, personal utilization, and classification ability. If you graph your consultants' responses, the experts often end up on the edges of the graph, while the nonexperts usually clump into a central group of "common knowledge" that most people know. By comparing experts and nonexperts, you can gather not just the in-depth information, but also see the patterns of "what most people know/think."

Collecting Data on Cultural Domains

The purpose of research design is to determine which of the available methods best gather the data necessary to fulfill one's research goals. The function, then, of research methods, or techniques, is to gather *pertinent,* or *salient* data—the information that can be used to answer your research questions and test your hypotheses. Several standard techniques are available to gather such data. The techniques described here include: (1) For eliciting lists of the items that belong in a domain: various types of free listing, and (2) for understanding how items within domains relate to each other and are organized: pile sorting, triads, paired comparisons, and frame substitutions. In addition, approaches that have been found useful for studying intracultural variation within domains are discussed, including cultural consensus analysis, qualitative text analysis, and quantitative text analysis. The first step, and the one that forms the foundation of the descriptive process, is to elicit the items within the domains being investigated.

Methodological Approaches to Sampling Cultural Domains

1. Free Listing

Free listing stands alone as a first step technique. Free list data can be used for many tasks where consultants are asked to manipulate or arrange a set if items. Free listing is used to gather the names of the items within a domain. The members of a domain are things that belong together in a group. Unlike the other methods, free listing does not give relational data of how the items in the list are organized, but additional steps can be added to listing to do this.

Free listing as a technique is easy and inexpensive to construct. You simply ask consultants to fill the domain for you by listing all of the kinds of ——. For example, ask: "Can you please list all of the foods you eat at thanksgiving dinner?" Free listing is easy to administer because the consultants can easily understand what information is requested of them (Figure 3.1). You ask several people, expert and nonexpert, to free list items in the same domain and then compare and compile their lists. It has the advantage of letting you elicit the membership of items (plants, foods, traits, weapons, tools, terms, holidays, etc . . .) in a domain. Several simple techniques can help you evaluate the *saliency* (relative importance) of items in the domain via frequency, rank order, and paired associations. When you combine the lists of several people, many items will be listed by several (sometimes all) of the consultants while others are listed by only a few or one. The frequency of each item is an indicator of its salience, as is its relative rank on the lists. For example, if you have students free list types of blue jeans, "Levi's" may not be the first type of jeans listed by each student, but it will be on the most of the students' lists. Levi's jeans are highly salient. They would be even more salient if they

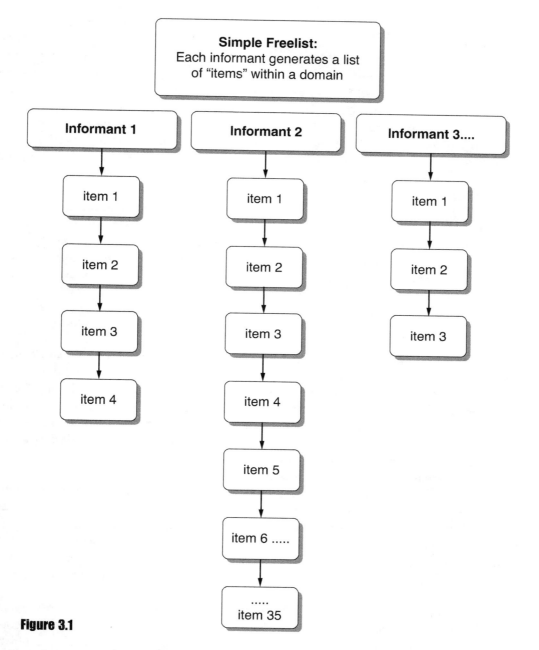

Figure 3.1

were the first or second type of jeans listed as well. A brand of jeans listed by only one or two students and appeared very low on the list of those students would not be as salient.

As you can see, salience is relative and used to compare items within the same domain. The sample used is an important determinant in the items gathered by free listing, so a careful researcher should be careful to sample people who are representative of the cultural group in question and to also sample enough people. It often surprises beginning researchers that an adequate sample size for free listing does not need to be very large. Twenty to thirty individuals can be sufficient, especially if several experts are included. As few as five-ten experts may give an exhaustive list, though this smaller sample will not have the same salience scores as lists collected from "average" members of the population because experts know so many items and tend to think quite differently than nonexperts in a field. (Remember, nonexperts are more likely to represent "common knowledge", but they are often very inaccurate compared to the experts.) After the lists start to become redundant, containing the same items with few or no new discovered, the free list sample is usually considered large enough. This often happens at around thirty individuals from within the same cultural and subcultural group.

Free listing is often the very useful "first step" in further exploration of a domain. Although free listing does not tell you how the members of a domain are cognitively arranged, it does let you construct the tools that will allow you to discover that information. The data from a free list can be used to construct tasks like pile sorts, triads, frame substitutions (using both items and traits of those items), paired comparisons, and numerous types of survey questions. In addition, free lists can reveal important or unique items that warrant further investigation through either structured tasks like those listed above or open-ended questions.

Other Types of Free Lists

A variation on the free list method is successive free listing, described by Gery Ryan (Ryan et al. 1999). Successive free listing builds upon an initial or primary simple free list to reveal further information about each item on that initial free list (Figure 3.2). After having a consultant generate a free list, the interviewer then goes back and asks another free list question of each of the items from the primary free list. The next step is attaching another, successive, free list to each of the items on the secondary list. The successive free list method branches away from the primary free list in an ever-branching, treelike network.

Another variation on a simple free list is to return to the items in a primary free list in a non-successive way. In this method, which I refer to as spoked free listing, you begin by having consultants generate a free list. For each of the items on that primary free list, a series of questions is asked. While the questions may be secondary free lists as in successive free listing, they may also include ratings or yes/no questions. For instance, after students listed types of blue jeans above, they could be asked to go back and rate whether each type of blue jean was "cool" or "geeky", "cheap" or "classy", to simply rate them on some scale of 1–10, or even to rank the items in their own list by various criteria. Alternatively, behaviors could be studied by asking the students to mark how often or whether they wear that type of jeans. Perceptions about social standing and customs could be gathered by asking students a judgmental question like "what type of people wear x type of jeans?" It is easy to see how a simple list could be used to gather much useful and interesting information about a domain.

For a spoked free list, each question in the series, however, returns to the item from the primary list (Figure 3.3). The most useful function of this method is that it allows the researcher to ask different categorization questions about the primary free list items. This allows a better understanding of domains where the items have multiple subdomains or belong to multiple groupings.

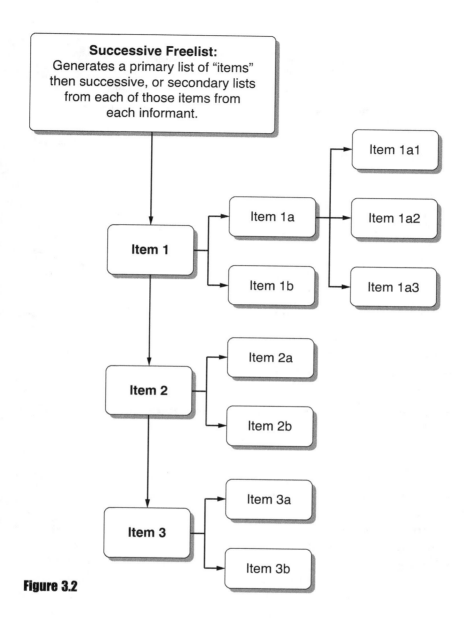

Figure 3.2

2. Gathering Relational Data

Once the ethnographer has a list of items in a domain, more testing can be done to gather data on how the items relate to one another. Pile sorting, triads, paired comparisons, and frame substitutions are techniques designed to reveal relational data on the items within a domain. In short, they are used to discover how people think about things in a domain or arrange/organize the information in their minds. Each is suited to different particular situations or questions, and has subtle differences. In general, you use them to discover how individuals perceptually arrange, group, or relate

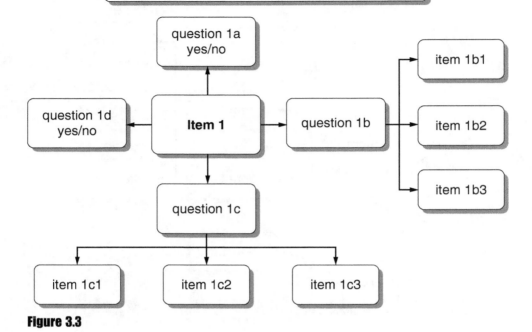

Figure 3.3

items. You can also determine what the important characteristics are for group membership. The data gathered allows a researcher to discover the classification system people use for that domain. Pile sorting is the most commonly used of the tasks designed to reveal relational data.

In pile sorting, consultants are simply asked to arrange items or representations of items in either a constrained (you tell them how many piles to make) or an unconstrained manner. You can either use real items such as birds, insects, bottles, etc . . ., or slips of paper with representations of items in the form of words, photos, or illustrations. The important detail in this technique is to remember to only place one thing or concept per card. Unlike the other techniques, you have the choice of having the consultant do a single pile sort or successive pile sorts. You can allow the consultant to 1) arrange the items in alternate patterns at the same level or 2) arrange each successive pile into further subdivided piles to obtain a hierarchical taxonomy. After the consultant sorts the items into piles, you record the items in each pile and ask the consultant to tell you the name of each pile and the criteria used to include or exclude things from each pile. A pile sort can be combined with a rating or ranking task. Rating tasks have consultants rate each item on a scale (usually of most to least) while ranking tasks have the consultants rank items within each pile. When you have a consultant pile sort, you are asking them to physically demonstrate how they classify the items in their minds.

Frame substitutions, also called sentence frames or frame elicitation, produce yes/no or true/false data. Their name comes from the fact that they are structured as the frames of sentences like "can _x_ come from _y_?" or "treatment _x_ is a good treatment for illness _y_." The ethnographer inserts items from two lists—a list of _x_'s and a list of _y_'s—gathered from free lists. By asking a series of these questions for all of your terms, you can measure differences between individual culture and shared culture. Compared to the other methods, they are especially suited to determining causative relationships and as such are a welcome resolution to the vagueness of meaning provided by statistical correlations. With a frame substitution, you can explicitly ask consultants how items are related. Frame substitutions are appropriate for smaller lists than the pile sorts, but differ in that you compare two classes of items (2 lists) to each other pairwise. Though frame substitutions gather a lot of precise data, they can be repetitive and tedious for consultants if you ask them to complete too many.

Pile sorts are best for gathering relational data about domains with lots of items because they do not feel as repetitive or tedious to consultants. It is generally believed that consultants like pile sorting and rarely consider it boring (Borgatti 1999, Boster 1994). Asking why piles go together, what they are, and combining other techniques like ranking and rating can reveal wealth of information. Though it does not yield the same quantitative data as other relational techniques, the richness of the qualitative data and the wealth of information keep pile sorting a popular and very useful option. Problems with pile sorting can occur with the natural tendency of some people to be lumpers or splitters. This problem occurs in free (unconstrained) pile sorts. You can address this by choosing constrained pile sorts. A constrained pile sort is where you specify how many piles a consultant can have, preventing them from trying to place everything in one or two piles (lumpers) or each item in it's own pile (splitters.) A lot of the variation in pile sorting can also be due to the nature of your stimulus. Photos, actual objects, and other representations of domain items can cause on-the-spot categorization based upon traits or form of the stimulus, not long term cultural beliefs about the items. Stephen Borgatti (1999) recommends being as abstract as possible if you want to elicit cultural beliefs, not sorting ability. Pile sorts are a great way to test the common reaction to domain items you gathered from your freelists.

Frame substitutions usually require computer software for analysis. An old but standard program called ANTHROPAC is often used. The ANTHROPAC yes/no x times y matrix is the easiest way to perform this analysis. There are many good ethnographic software programs available now, and the adventurous researcher can even write their own formulae for numerous other statistical software packages. In ANTHROPAC, simply adding several matrices (1 per consultant) allows you to get multidimensional scaling. Very good for particular types of data, especially causative factors in medical anthropology, frame substitutions were used in classic anthropological studies by L. Garro (1986), who measured folk medical knowledge, by J. Boster (1986) in distinguishing manioc cultivars among the Aguaruna, and Chavez et al. (1995) in their exploration of cancer risk factors. The individual questions, presented one at a time, are fairly quick and easy for consultants, but they become tedious and boring. For just 25 animals and 25 attributes, or descriptors, you have $25 \times 25 = 625$ questions! If you want to include frame substitutions in your research design, you must be sure the domains, items, attributes, etc . . . are culturally relevant, small, and make sense or the consultants won't tolerate the questions and will become biased due to fatigue.

Theoretical Approaches for Studying Intracultural Variation

There are a variety of approaches for thinking about intracultural variation within domains. Important and widely used approaches for studying knowledge in anthropology include Cultural Consensus Analysis, conceptualizing knowledge and intracultural variation as a combination of particle and wave models, the simple wave model of knowledge, and a combination of qualitative text analysis and quantitative text analysis. In particular, researchers choose among these approaches because of the different ways they identify experts and nonexperts. If you want to learn more, references to important scholars in these areas are listed at the end of the chapter.

1. Cultural Consensus

An important construct in cultural anthropology, intracultural variation is closely associated with the concepts of experts, nonexperts, and cultural consensus modeling. Each of these terms is defined and explained in terms of the structure and content of cultural domains. Intracultural variation is simply the variation that exists among the individuals within a culture (Bernard 1995). Variation within culture can occur along several lines. Some variation among individuals is to be expected, since a single individual does not hold the sum total of a culture's contents. Knowledge can be distributed among individuals as a part of their individual attributes. Variation also occurs between subgroups within a culture, wherein members of the same group have more overlap or consensus in their knowledge than members of larger cultural groupings.

A standard way of measuring and revealing intracultural variation is analysis of the differences in free list content and length. Cognitive differences have been measured by comparing relational organization with triads, pile sorts, frame substitution tests, rankings, ratings, and paired comparisons. Cultural consensus modeling, described by Romney et al. (1986, 1987) is a method for determining "cultural knowledge" that attempts to quantitatively demonstrate 1) an estimate of cultural competence, or knowledge level, for each consultant and 2) how to infer "correct" answers. Cultural consensus modeling attempts to meet these two goals on the basis of the belief that knowledge can be inferred from consensus among a sample of people. According to this model, consultants who are more competent (more expert) will have higher consensus and more culturally "correct" answers in their domain of expertise. In order for Consensus Analysis to be valid, it is assumed that for a domain:

1. There is a common truth, or fixed answer in shared cultural reality.

2. There is local independence, and consultant-item responses are random variables that satisfy conditional independence (conditional on the correct answer key.)

3. Items are homogenous, so all questions have the same difficulty level for all consultants

Analysis with cultural consensus modeling creates measures of cultural competence (variables symbolized by "D's") that allow the researcher to compare the competence of the consultants.

Since these estimates are comparable to other groups' or cultures' measures, one can compare among groups as well as within groups.

Consensus analysis also allows the identification of experts and nonexperts, or novices, in particular domains by the differences in their free list length (# items displayed in domain.) Experts are expected to have more items in their domain of expertise, and to be able to name both the highly salient (for the entire group) items and a number of unique items not known to novices. Nonexperts, by contrast, are those with smaller domains centered on a few core items that are typically either highly salient to them or highly ubiquitous in their society.

In relational exercises like pile sorts, triads, and paired comparisons, experts are expected to have greater consistency as well as greater sophistication in organization than novices. This sophistication, or "expertise", is based upon the assumptions of cultural consensus modeling. In consensus modeling, if there is a "correct" answer, then experts are those with more consistently correct answers according to the sample group's most common answers. Weller (1984) used four measures of consensus under the cultural consensus model to identify experts: 1) reliability, 2) overall consensus, 3) degree of consensus, and 4) index of competency. All four of these measures are based upon the assumptions that consensus is "correct", and that the most culturally competent consultants are those that agree the most with the other individuals in the sample group.

The problem with this is that many types of knowledge are not democratic. For example, most people in 15th century Europe believed that the Earth was flat. Did this make it true? Experts have much more training in their area of expertise than nonexperts. Take, for instance, an exam in your chemistry or genetics class. If most of the class answered question #3 as answer B, does this make it correct even though correct answer is A according to the knowledge held by the professor and textbook? *According to the Cultural Consensus Model, the most average person is the most expert.* This is very useful for finding information for marketing or language research, but not for technical information. Think carefully about your research questions and the type of research you are conducting when you choose an approach to understanding intracultural variation and determining expertise.

2. Alternatives to the Cultural Consensus Model

Of course, there is another way that experts and novices are identified in research. Outside of consensus modeling, experts are often labeled by their roles. Physicians, medicine men, and other health care practitioners, for example, are expected to be experts in medicine. Ph.D.s in botany and zoology are expected to be experts in plant and animal domains, respectively. Experts are not necessarily people who agree the most with everyone. Instead, experts are individuals with a great deal of training and/or experience in a domain. People without any apparent special training or exposure to the finer details of a particular domain are assumed to be nonexperts since they are not expected to have any pragmatic reason for expertise.

Experts may also be identified by the snowball technique. For example, in my herbal medicine research, I located few initial experts via their professions on the assumption that licensed practitioners would be experts. In exploratory, informal conversations and interviews, I asked these initial experts to recommend other experts for my sample group. In addition, members of a subculture can be asked to identify the acknowledged experts in their group. As another example, I asked members of the populations I sampled from who they considered to be experts and who they used or recommended as herbal practitioners. Searching within likely contexts such as subcultures, venues, or environments experts are likely to frequent allows a narrower search for potential consultants.

Jim Boster (1987) used an approach to intracultural variation that is more balanced. He agrees with proponents of the Cultural Consensus Model that by understanding how individuals learn, remember and transmit cultural knowledge you can understand how cultures work. He also believes that you should study how individuals vary to build models of how collective understandings emerge from individual learning. Within this field, though, there is a disagreement over what the patterning of intracultural variation. Intracultural variation is the pattern of disagreement among members of a community across a variety of domains.

There are two theories, or models, of how consultant knowledge can be described. Boster calls these two models **particle theory** and **wave theory.** *The particle theory* holds that knowledge is coherent, in discrete pieces actively constructed into models that add up in more knowledgeable people. Learning in particle theory, thing would be individual. The cultural consensus model is a particle theory of knowledge.

The *wave theory* proposes that different individuals have different pieces of the picture, passively acquired, and sets of rules about knowledge that allow them to deal with novel situations. People would learn from the social or physical environment. D'Andrade (1987), proposes the wave theory of knowledge. For example, D'Andrade used word association tests, which have no single correct answer. He found that subjects choosing modal word association responses had higher IQs, better education, and were more reliably knowledgeable. Expertise is based upon an individual's ability to understand, recall, and manipulate knowledge, not the ability to supply the most popular answer.

Boster points out that both approaches work. In addition, a combination of the two approaches could be the best of all. Because I had a high number of experts in my sample, which will be at a disadvantage in consensus analysis, the alternative "wave" approach would allow a more balanced analysis of my consultants.

In this study I could keep the valuable idea of consensus while using methods more aligned with wave theory to better suit my research questions, sample, and data.

In a classic example, Chavez et al. (1995) measured intracultural or at least subcultural variation across two domains using free lists, frame substitution tests, and ranking. They compared perceived risk factors for breast and cervical cancer and their importance among 5 groups (Latinas, Mexican women, Salvadoran women, Anglo women, and physicians). They found that different groups had different models of risk and different patterning of those models. They were able to conclude that even in the same main culture, different subcultural groups have different understanding of knowledge. This study was an interesting model for my own research, since I am looking at different groups within Western culture with differing yet perhaps overlapping perceptions of health care. Especially informative are Chavez et al.'s methods. The women supplied their own risk factors (free list), and the rankings, frame substitutions, and pile sorts were based upon this data.

Limitations of Some Approaches

1. Potential Problems in Gathering Domain Information

Free lists reveal variation both within and among groups. The groups may be at whatever level you decide as long as you use the appropriate technique to separate/distinguish them.

"Loose talk and the freedom of free lists"

Despite its utility, there are a number of problems with free list analysis. First and foremost, there is great variation in the salience of items within a domain by gender, occupation, and frequency of utilization of items within a domain. Another problem with using free lists is the "loose talk phenomenon" discovered by Gatewood (1983) in which people often know the names of things with which they are not truly familiar. Some consultants may have a long list, but that list may be quite shallow, with little knowledge about the items listed. For example, by pairing a secondary free list and yes/no questions about use and recommendation to each plant given in the herbal remedy free list, I hoped to offset the problem of the loose talk phenomenon. A comparison of the size of free list size to 1) percent of items used, 2) percent of items recommended, and 3) length of uses for those remedies should show the comparative "shallowness" of knowledge among consultants. In addition to the loose talk phenomenon, consultants may simply make up things to appear more knowledgeable in front of the ethnographer. This source of error may be difficult to discern in situations with sample populations utilizing knowledge from a variety of sources. As discussed earlier, the defining natures of inventions of tradition and revitalization movements make it very likely that unreferencable or vague information sources will be given. Because these sources are vague or not readily available for verification and assessment, it may be very difficult to discern which items were made up on the spot by creative and eager-to-impress consultants.

Pile sorts have both advantages and disadvantages. Pile sorts have the advantage of revealing the differences and similarities in how different consultants organize and relate items within the domain. You can also elicit consultant names and reasons for individual categorizations. Successive pile sorts therefore allow you to build individual taxonomies for each consultant in order to compare them. In addition to this, there are several other perceived advantages to pile sorts. Pile sorts are generally believed by anthropologists to be pleasant, easily understood, and quick for consultants. In addition, pile sorts generate a wealth of *direct* information about *why* certain groupings are made. The less constrained format that should allow a relaxed flow of information with consultants that may make them comfortable and talkative. Pile sort data are more complex to analyze quantitatively, however, and tend to be described in more qualitative terms.

Experts are too "Expert" for Pile Sorting

The tradeoff for the complexity and difficulty in analyzing pile sorts is the richness of the information they provide on hierarchical relationships among items. Pile sorts, then, are particularly good for deriving an indirect data to construct a model of the classification of the items within a domain by the hierarchical relationships among items generated by successive pile sorts. However, there are problems with using pile sorts with some types of consultants. While perceived by anthropologists to be fun and easy for many consultants, pile sorts can be quite frustrating to experts for performance, professional, and cultural reasons. The frustration of experts may be explained by D'Andrade's (1987) wave theory of knowledge. Because experts are familiar enough with knowledge within their domain of expertise to manipulate it in a number of ways, they can construct several *alternate* ways to sort the items. Their frustration may result from a desire to understand *which* type of organization is requested. Pile sorts may be better suited to nonexperts and non-professional experts, (i.e. those who are not professionally trained or practitioners in the domain).

My personal experience with interviewing experts provides more insight into expert frustration with pile sorting. Evidence for the wave theory explanation of experts frustration is found in the behavior of experts during pile sorting tasks. Experts have sufficient knowledge of all of the elements of their system that they continually ask "how" or "which way" of sorting is desired. Even though eager to be helpful, the expert has so many ways of manipulating the items that they take a long time to perform all of the possible sortings and become fatigued. Experts may experience frustration at both the seemingly endless task of multiple pile sorts and the difficulty in choosing just one way of organizing the items. This becomes a serious issue in ethnographic research because experts, time is often limited, and they don't want to take a long time doing interview tasks.

2. Potential Problems Limiting the Usefulness of the Cultural Consensus Model

Any analysis using the Cultural Consensus Model is vulnerable to error if the assumptions of the cultural consensus model are broken. There are several assumptions of cultural consensus modeling, given in Romney et al (1986, 1987). The three most fundamental were discussed above. There are other assumptions in cultural consensus modeling that could cause problems when investigating intracultural diversity, however. First, the interview subject is assumed to be a situation where ethnographer does not know either how much each consultant knows about a cultural domain or the answers to the questions. One expects a correspondence between answers of consultants that is a function of the extent to which each answer is correlated with the cultural truth. This is what allows you to identify experts. Outliers are weighted less because it is assumed that they are not as knowledgeable or "correct" about a single, fixed true "answer" that should apply to all consultants.

Experts by definition tend to know more and different knowledge than nonexperts. Because of the assumptions of consensus as "correctness" on items, experts are at a disadvantage in consensus analysis and frequently score very low (Boster 1987). By contrast, consultants who know only a few items of high ubiquity are scored as the most culturally competent. This is exactly the opposite of most of the goals of studies of expert knowledge.

Cultural consensus modeling goes on to assume consultants don't guess and are independent. If consultants are obtaining their knowledge from the same source (such as an influential book), they will not be independent. The consultants may share some values, but all of the groups don't share single belief system. Consultants may also guess in order to quickly give an answer and move on.

Summary

In conclusion, many issues need to be considered before choosing data collection techniques. The cultural appropriateness of the methods, the specific information needed to meet research objectives, and the optimum balance between maintaining rapport and efficiently gathering data should all be factors in the final structuring of the research design. Background research to generate initial research questions guides the rest of the project design. Participant observation and informal interviews helps the ethnographer to establish rapport with the people in the culture to be studied and helps him or her to write better questions and choose methods that will be appropriate. Collecting oral histories and personal narratives from consultants provides rich information about the culture in the words of the people being studied. More specific data can be collected on cultural domains of interest with free lists. While free listing seems to be a robust technique appropriate to most if not all populations, other followup methods using the lists generated should be chosen to suit what the data and the population being studied. A mixture of rankings, pile sorting, ratings, survey questions, and frame substitutions may be chosen as needed. In some populations, other methods of obtaining the organizational data should be utilized as an alternative to pile sorting in order to avoid offending consultants to whom it would be uncomfortable for cultural or professional reasons. Carefully weigh your need for data to meet research objectives with the needs and feelings of your consultants. Time spent in participant observation and discussion with consultants about their comfort level with interview tasks may reveal potential problem methods and solutions to your research problems.

Name _____ Date _____

I. Learning More About Fieldwork and Ethnographic Methods:

Assignment A: Basic Terms and Concepts from Ethnography

1. How does ethnographic fieldwork performed by anthropologists differ from other types of scientific data collection?

_____

_____

_____

2. What is **ethnography**?

_____

_____

_____

3. What is **participant observation?**

_____

_____

_____

4. Why is it important to consider the difference between the terms *informant* and *consultant?* Which would you rather be called?

_____

_____

_____

5. Why is *subject* not an appropriate term for the people anthropologists study?

_____

_____

_____

6. What is the difference between an *expert* and a *nonexpert*? Define each.

_____

_____

_____

7. Give an example of an expert and the criteria for deciding that person is an expert.

_____

_____

_____

8. What is a **freelist** and how is it created?

_____

_____

_____

9. What is a **domain**? Define.

_____

_____

_____

10. What can you learn about a culture from studying domains?

_____

_____

_____

11. What is **quantitative** data? Give an example of a type of quantitative data.

_____

_____

_____

12. What is **qualitative** data? Give an example of a type of qualitative data.

_____

_____

_____

13. What is **consensus** in ethnographic data, and how important is it among your research sample?

_____

_____

_____

Assignment B: Practicing with Domains

In the table below, give an example of a domain and the items that would be placed inside it.

Name of Domain:	
	Items in this domain. . . .
1	
2	
3	
4	
5	
6	
7	
8	
9	
10	

Name _____ Date _____

II. Practicing Ethnographic Methods: Freelists

Assignment A: Design a Freelist Exercise

Think of another domain. Write the name of your domain here _____

For this domain, think of one where you know both an expert and a nonexpert. For example, you may choose a topic from one of your classes, where you could ask your professor to be the expert and a fellow student to be the nonexpert. You might use one of your parents or boss as an expert.

Who is your expert? _____ How did you determine that this person was

an expert? _____

Ask the expert to list items in your domain on the form below.

	Name of Domain: Items in this domain. . . .
1	
2	
3	
4	
5	
6	
7	
8	
9	
10	

Name _____ Date _____

Who is your nonexpert? _____ How did you determine that this person

was a nonexpert? _____

Ask the nonexpert to list items in your domain on the form below.

	Name of Domain:
	Items in this domain. . . .
1	
2	
3	
4	
5	
6	
7	
8	
9	
10	

Assignment B: Interpreting and Analyzing Freelist Data
Compare the two lists.

1. Who listed more items?

_____

_____

_____

2. How did the things listed by the expert differ from the nonexpert list?

_____

_____

_____

3. How did the expert act while listing compared to the nonexpert?

_____

_____

_____

4. What does this experience tell you about nonexperts and experts?

_____

_____

_____

Assignment C: More Advanced Uses of Freelists

For more advanced practice, you can expand your sample to include more experts and nonexperts. You can also have your consultants manipulate the freelist data. The activities below are exercises that will help you to manipulate freelists for more data.

Have your consultants do the following:

Ranking and Defining Freelist Items:

For the items listed in your freelist, please:

- rank them in order of most important to least important (*write the "rank" number beside each item*)

- tell me which of the items is the most typical, or representative example of a _____ (insert name of the domain)?

- mark which items you "like," "dislike," or are neutral about

Manipulating Freelist Items:

Gather the items from all of your freelists. Write them on index cards and shuffle them. Hand the stack of cards to your consultant and have them sort them into piles as a way of organizing or categorizing the items.

Ask your consultant to tell you the names of his/her piles (pile sorting). Then ask them to explain why they categorized them that way.

You can also use the cards for ranking or other manipulative tasks.

Your instructor may have you design more advanced exercises for data collection.

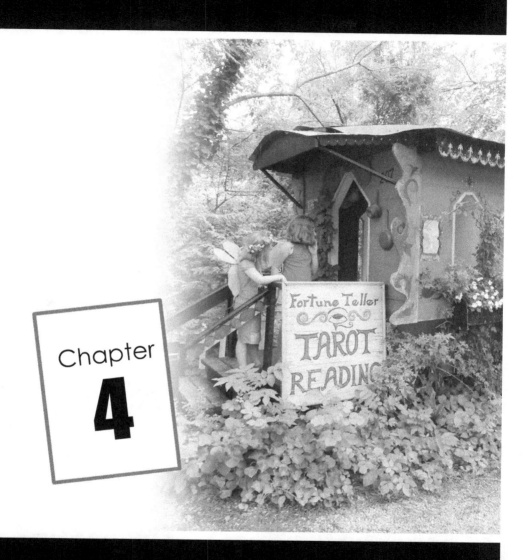

Chapter

4

Research Design: An Overview of the Project

Research Population and Sample Terms

The best laid plans for research often change dramatically once you go into the field. As said in the preface, this book allows me to present information gathered during my dissertation research into the use of herbal remedies by Americans. My original research questions were focused on why people choose herbal remedies, and my pilot projects showed that a high concentration of herbal remedy experts, practitioners, and consumers were reenactors. So, I designed my fieldwork to gather ethnographic data from herbal remedy users in reenactment groups among others.

In my search for individuals using and practicing traditional European herbal medicine, I studied historical reenactors because they were part of the field environment. In the process, I became more and more interested in reenactment culture as I learned more about it. Though I began by studying the culture of herbal remedies, I ended up being drawn into an investigation of reenactment culture as well. I added new research questions and expanded my observation, participant observation, and data collection to gather ethnographic data on reenactors as a subculture.. not just the herbal remedy use. It evolved into a new ethnographic study. Most of my fieldwork was with members of the S.C.A., but curiosity and a need for cross-cultural comparison led me to investigate and interview members of other reenactment genres as well. The following chapter describes the research sampled to provide interview data for this project as well as the environment of that fieldwork. Since then, I have continued to study and observe reenactors, especially Renaissance Faire reenactors and Civil War reenactors. Since the first writing of this book, I've done cross-cultural comparisons with other types of reenactors (fantasy reenactors), role play groups (LARPers, cosplay), and paracultures.

The first section includes information about the people interviewed as consultants for the study. Background information for consultants includes their demographic information, affiliations, and the sampling method by which they were identified for interviewing. Next, the environment and setting of the interviews is described; and lessons learned from the fieldwork are described.

Sampling Structure

The sampling structure is displayed in Tables 4.1 and 4.2. A total of 42 consultants were interviewed, subdivided into: 1) 10 herbal practitioners and 17 herbal consumers from the herbal remedies research project, and 2) 16 additional reenactors who were not selected as herbal remedy consultants. Consultants were assured anonymity, so their names were replaced with anonymous codes identifying their groupings

Every detail is important on reproduction garments. Period-authentic laces, ties, and toggles are used.
Copyright Jupiter Images.

Table 4.1—*Consultants originally chosen for interview for herbal remedy use, but who identified themselves as reenactors. "Practitioners" are experts who practice as herbalists. "Consumers" are people who consumed at least 3 types herbal remedies regularly.*

Groupings	Expertise	Anonymous Code	Gender	Age Group	Sample Context
Practitioners	European herbal medicine	PE02	Female	40-45	S.C.A. event, self-identified
	"	PE03	Female	50-55	S.C.A. event, rec by other expert
	"	PE04	Female	25-30	Rennaissance Faire, self-identified
	"	PE05	Female	30-35	Rennaissance Faire, self-identified
	Modern/Ecclectic herbal medicine	PM01	Female	35-40	rec by consumer
	"	PM03	Female	45-50	self-identified, alternative bookstore
	"	PM04	Male	40-45	rec by practitioner
	"	PM07	Male	50-55	Alternative bookstore, self-identified
	"	PM08	Female	35-40	Alternative bookstore, rec by consumer
	"	PM09	Female	35-40	S.C.A. event, rec by consumer
Consumers	nonexpert	C10	Female	55-60	S.C.A. event
	"	C11	Male	30-35	S.C.A. event
	"	C12	Male	50-55	S.C.A. event
	"	C13	Male	50-55	S.C.A. event
	"	C15	Female	25-30	S.C.A. event
	"	C19	Male	35-40	Rennaissance Faire
	"	C20	Female	30-35	Wiccan coven
	"	C27	Female	20-24	Alternative bookstore, Wiccan coven
	"	C29	Male	35-40	Rennaissance Faire
	"	C30	Male	45-50	Rennaissance Faire
	"	C31	Female	30-35	Alternative bookstore
	"	C33	Female	50-55	S.C.A. event, rec by practitioner
	expertise in herbal medicine	CE06	Female	30-35	self-identified, Wiccan coven
	"	CE07	Female	25-30	S.C.A. self-identified
	"	CE08	Female	25-30	self-identified, Wiccan coven
	"	CE14	Female	40-45	S.C.A. event
	"	CE16	Female	35-40	S.C.A. event

Table 4.2—*Additional consultants interviewed about reenactment participation and culture.*

Anonymous Code	Gender	Age Group	Sample Context
SCA01	Male	30–35	S.C.A. event
SCA02	Male	25–30	S.C.A. event
SCA03	Male	30–35	S.C.A. event, Rennaissance Faire
SCA04	Female	30–35	S.C.A. event
SCA05	Female	45–50	S.C.A. event, Rennaissance Faire
SCA06	Female	40–45	S.C.A. event
RNF01	Male	40–45	Rennaissance Faire, Rendezvous
RNF02	Female	30–35	Rennaissance Faire
RNF03	Female	20–25	Rennaissance Faire, S.C.A.
RNF04	Female	18–20	Rennaissance Faire
RNF05	Female	18–20	Rennaissance Faire, S.C.A.
RNF06	Female	20–25	Rennaissance Faire, S.C.A.
RDV01	Male	50–55	Rendezvous
CW01	Male	45–50	Civil War, living history
CW02	Male	40–45	Civil War, Rendezvous
CW03	Male	45–50	Civil War, Texas Republican

and an individual number. Additional data was gathered from participant observation, observation, informal conversations, and literature review.

In this experimental study, most of my consultants were experts at reenacting, though many were considered much more "expert" than others by both their own evaluation and by their peers. Because this was a study specifically to know more about reenacting, not the general public's thoughts or common knowledge about reenactors, I needed to interview reenactors to get accurate information. For the last decade, however, as I've been teaching from this project, I've gathered quite a bit of observational and educational data about nonexpert perceptions of and reactions to reenactors. (*Think of those introductory assignments with preconceptions people have about reenactors.*) It has helped tremendously in reframing the information about reenactors to make it more accessible to a general audience.

Research Populations and Environment

Consultants, in general, were located by the **snowball technique**. The **snowball technique** was described by Boster (1994), and is a simple but effective method of locating consultants by having consultants recommend others who would be good candidates for interview. Finding the initial consultants in each sample group, however, required other methods. The technique for finding consultants within each sample grouping is described below with the definitions for grouping terms. Demographic variables such as age, gender, ethnicity, and context were recorded for analysis, but because the snowball technique is not random, there were no preset goals of obtaining set numbers of these sociodemographic categories. I did have minimum quotas for several of the groupings, a minimum of 5 experts each in Native American, Traditional Chinese medicine, European traditional, and Modern/Ecclectic herbalism and a minimum of 15 nonexperts in herbal medicine. Then, 3 experts each in civil war, S.C.A. and RenFaire reenacting. Because the original goal of my fieldwork was to research herbal remedy use, many of my consultants were chosen or recommended because of their knowledge of herbal remedies. As I searched for more information on reenactment culture in general instead of herbal remedies in particular, I interviewed other reenactors without regard to their knowledge on herbs. The only interviews included in this data are from reenactors. Because I was interested in reenactors from an emic point of view, I only interviewed individuals who stated that they participated in reenacting.

To identify individuals for interview in the original fieldwork, I relied on a variety of simple techniques. Often I initiated conversation about an individual's garb, artifacts, or merchandise to establish preliminary rapport and evaluate the individual's knowledge of herbal remedies (or later, reenacting). Once this was done, and the individuals were at ease, I simply asked "Can you recommend anyone who is an expert in herbs?", or "Do you know anyone who could tell me more about reenacting?" Employees at alternative bookstores; people in small shops or merchant stalls with displays of locally produced herbal products, historical-period supplies (one knitting/and wool supply vendor was particularly helpful); and a variety of other merchants were very fruitful areas to gather information. In addition to finding individuals to formally interview, many of these informal encounters filled my notebooks with data about the habits, customs, and material culture of reenactors. Additional consultants were obtained by simply asking people around the University of Missouri campus if they would be interested in completing a short interview. In the campus setting, many individuals are quite willing to participate in interview projects, whether they are students, faculty, or staff. For the second edition of this book, I conducted additional research specifically with reenactors, interviewing more reenactors and doing additional fieldwork, observation, and participant observation.

Interview Environment

Interviews were conducted in either private, semi-private, or public settings at the preference of the consultant. We sought a location that was comfortable to the consultant, such as their office, tent, home, or a neutral location such as a coffee shop. Both the consultant and I sat and faced each other during the interviews.

Interview schedules were used to guide interviews and ensure that all questions were answered. Potential consultants were allowed to see a summary of the interview structure and questions to determine whether they felt comfortable with the interview process and subject matter. Once consultants agreed to the interview, a time for the interview was scheduled. While some consultants scheduled a later appointment for the interview, many immediately began the interview. At the beginning of the actual interview, consultants were given an informed consent form approved by the University of Missouri Internal Research Board Human Subjects Committee. This form contained contact information for the university, the MU Anthropology Department, my advisor, and myself. Consultants were also given a business card with my contact information. To complete this book, some consultants were recontacted and asked follow-up questions. Only informants who had indicated at the time of their interview that they wished to be contacted at a future date were recontacted. Since the original research, additional work with reenactors was conducted at Stephen F. Austin State University, with interviews conforming to Human Subjects regulations and Institutional Review Board approval of interview materials.

Interview Tools

Interview information was recorded with pencil and paper onto empty data recording sheets or onto a small reporter's-style notepad. When permission was given by the consultant, the interviews were recorded on an audio tape in a micro cassette recorder. Interview information from these forms and tapes was recorded directly into Excel spreadsheets.

If the consultant consented, a camera loaded with 35 mm slide film and/or standard photographic film was used to take photographs of the interview settings as well as artifacts the consultants used or constructed. During or after the interview, consultants frequently wished to show me favorite artifacts. Fieldwork since the first edition used digital recorders and cameras.

Interview Experiences

Individual differences existed among the consultants, often typical of a particular subgroup. Pilot studies are great for discovering patterns in your research population or site, but sometimes you still get surprises in the field. For instance, I conducted several interviews with Native American herbal practitioners which were quite different from the other interviews in my research. I had to adapt my training and methodology to perform the interviews in a way deemed culturally appropriate by members of the society. Before obtaining permission to perform an interview, I had to meet and converse with several individuals. These individuals 1) made recommendations to elders or practitioners about whether or not I should be seen, 2) provided helpful information for appropriate behavior, 3) evaluated my sincerity and willingness to listen, and 4) chose whether or not reveal themselves as practitioners or not during an initial conversation phase of the interviews. In many cases, particularly at PowWows or scheduled interviews, several other individuals were present or "dropped by". These individuals were a part of the evaluation process and often turned out to be practitioners themselves who were evaluating me incognito or their intermediaries. If the contact stated that they were not interested, I respected their wishes and did not pursue them further.

Four out of the five Native American practitioners I formally interviewed refused a tape recorder during the interview. Instead, I was required to demonstrate respect by conducting the interview in a traditional method. I was asked questions to determine my seriousness and background. Then I listened to the practitioner, asking the questions as prompts when it was requested or letting them select the question order. I could write down information, but performed appropriately by reciting the information back to them to demonstrate my understanding in a traditional learning method. If my repetition was incorrect, the practitioner corrected me and explained again to clarify. Personally, I found this to be a wonderful way of conducting interviews. Though I was initially flustered, since this is quite different from the training I received in methods classes and the literature, I rapidly adapted with the patience of my consultants. My own Native American heritage was an important factor in these interactions, as my face and features were scrutinized, and I was asked to provide information about my ancestry as my consultants searched for a common connection between us. That tenuous connection was often used by my consultants as a basis for rapport and recognizing me as distant kin who needed instruction in Native traditions.

The advantages of the format preferred by the Native American practitioners are many. The consultant has a comfortable role as teacher in the format with which they are familiar. In addition, both parties are able to ensure that ideas were clearly conveyed. These interviews were very satisfying for both parties and ensured that consultants did not feel like "test subjects" or "experimental objects/animals". I became the student, in many cases quite literally sitting on the ground at my consultant's knee to receive instruction from an elder.

Four of my European herbal practitioners rarely had the opportunity to perform professionally outside of their paracultural communities in the Society of Creative Anachronism or Renaissance Faires. They were quite friendly and willing to be interviewed, but not all potential practitioners were able to dedicate the time needed to conduct a full interview. Because they were uncomfortable performing outside their communities, these consultants were interviewed in either S.C.A. or Renaissance Faire settings and in their period persona.

The consultants were a little nervous about their performances, but comfortable and very willing to answer questions, often asking "Is there anything else I could tell you?" and encouraging their friends to "come and try it". This worked particularly well in the setting of the Society of Creative Anachronism events and Wiccan covens. Both sub-cultural groups value information and learning, and were quite eager to quiz *me* afterwards in order to obtain more information sources. As I've gotten more comfortable in reenacting communities, it often becomes easier to establish rapport and obtain interviews. There will always be people, however, who just don't want to be interviewed. Of course, there will also often be people who very much want to be interviewed. . . but who are not accepted as experts by the rest of their community. You have to decide what you are comfortable doing.

Every attempt is made to recreate the period feel or bed through use of artifacts and historic settings. Muskets and gear arranged in a Union camp.
Photo by Steve Shore.

Fieldwork Interaction with Sampled Populations

While interviews serve to collect data from consultants, less formal interaction with sampled populations is necessary to establish rapport. Participant observation is the ideal way to truly understand the emic perspective of the population you are studying, but true participant observation is not always possible. Less intense interactions with consultants include informal conversations, observation of activities, and establishment of friendship with key consultants. The question then becomes "Exactly how does one locate and establish contact with key consultants?" This question is particularly salient in research settings in the United States. While one could act like a news reporter from the evening news and stand about with a camera and notepad waiting for consultants to pass by, this is not the best way to obtain targeted sample groups. It is also not the best way to achieve the interactions necessary to establish rapport.

As discussed above, the first method I used was to frequent contexts which consultants were expected to frequent. These included providers/merchants who sold herbs and herbal remedies, supplies for period reproductions, and event merchants as well as cultural events where reenactors were gathered for living history demonstrations. Before I attempted to gain permission to conduct interview, I observed and interacted with reenactors in an informal way to learn more about typical activities and accepted behaviors. During this time, I talked informally with individuals, asking questions and generally becoming familiar with the environment. After identifying and establishing rapport with initial consultants, I was able to begin asking for interviews. I also observed and conversed with reenactors at PowWows, Society for Creative Anachronism events, Renaissance Faires, a Rendezvous event, living history demonstrations, and Civil War reenactments.

I was able to conduct participant observation at S.C.A. events and Renaissance Faires. With the assistance of a few key informants, I was able to achieve the immersion which typifies participant observation and that allowed me to participate in activities alongside my sample population as "one of them" at Society of Creative Anachronism events. Unlike a place of business or an event designed to demonstrate to an audience, these events stress the need for everyone to "remain period" by dressing, speaking, and behaving in the agreed-upon form of "the modern middle ages." The boundary line between the performers and audience is not present, since everyone is participating in the same activity—group play. Since these events exist in a discrete time period and location, the researcher can "go there" and stay in the participant observation mode for a prolonged period of up to 10 days. This was a valuable way to establish rapport that is much more like standard anthropological fieldwork methods than other contexts. During participant observation, I attended community activities and helped with tasks like food preparation, "riding the tents" during a thunderstorm, and dying cloth. I also attended ritual performances like "court" and "battles" as well as the classes on medieval and S.C.A.-related topics that are at the core of this re-enactment-oriented community. My participant observation experiences are discussed more in the sections on the S.C.A. and Renaissance Faires in the next section of the book.

Conclusions

In summary, I located and established rapport with members of my sample populations in a variety of context-specific ways. I was able to conduct participant observation with the S.C.A. group and interactions that included conversation, observation, and interviews with the other sample populations. The practice establishing rapport with the S.C.A. population had the added benefit of making it easier to establish rapport with individuals in the similar, if more demonstration-oriented atmosphere of the Renaissance Faires, Civil War and other living history reenactments, and Pow-Wows.

Name _____ Date_____

I. Learning More About Ethnography, Part 2:

In Chapter 2, you began an assignment to read and summarize an ethnography. This second part of the assignment is designed to help you *evaluate* that ethnography now that you have read more about ethnographic research.

For Part 2 of the assignment:

1. Describe the methods used by the ethnographer.

2. List any quantitative methods used and data gathered by the ethnographer.

3. List any qualitative methods used and data gathered by the ethnographer.

4. What research questions did the ethnographer begin with? Were each of these answered? List the questions and the ethnographer's answers for each.

5. Were the ethnographer's research questions revised as they worked? How?

_____

_____

_____

6. Did the ethnographer have any problems with their original research strategy? Describe the problems and any solutions the ethnographer tried.

_____

_____

_____

7. What new questions or hypotheses arise out of the fieldwork?

_____

_____

_____

8. Do you think the ethnographer was successful in choosing methods to answer their research questions? Explain.

_____

_____

_____

9. Finally, can you think of other methods or data you would have liked to have seen in this ethnography? Describe.

_____

_____

_____

II. Practicing Research Design

Assignments: Choosing a Research Question and Approach:

Look back to the listing assignments you completed in Chapter 1. What ethnographic method did you use? (Use the proper terms)

_____

Was this list qualitative or quantitative data? _____

Use your results (your data) to generate a research question about reenactors.

Question: _____

_____

Now, how can you answer your research question? Answer the questions below to help you develop a strategy.

Is your sample size of 2–3 consultants enough? _____ Explain.

_____

_____

_____

How would you use the methods you have seen and practiced in chapters 1–4 to gather the data you need? _____

_____

_____

_____

Name _____ Date _____

What data do you need and what method do you need to gather that data? Write your research plan.

_____

_____

_____

How will you use this data to decide on the answer for your research question?

_____

_____

_____

PART II

The Reenactors: Who Are They?

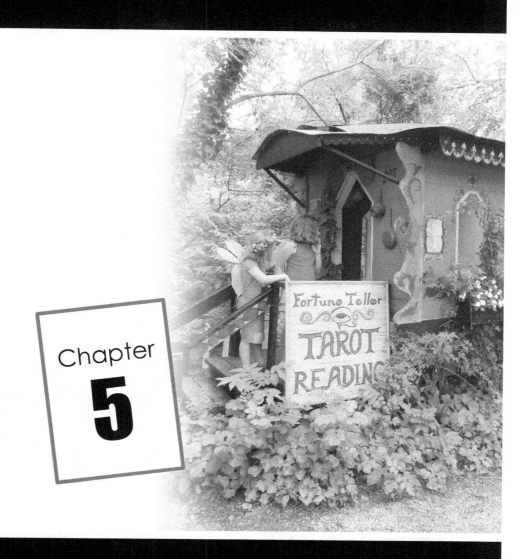

Chapter
5

Society for Creative Anachronism

The S.C.A.: It Started With a Party

It all started with a May Day theme party in Berkeley, California in 1966. The founding event was a May 1st tournament, and though the SCA did not incorporate formally until 1968, this event is considered the beginning of SCA reenacting. The idea caught on, and soon the SCA had spread around California and to college campuses around the U.S. Before long, the SCA was more than a college phenomenon. The "Known World", as the SCA's society and organized groups are known, now consists of 20 kingdoms with over 30,000 members around the world. Though formal membership in the SCA numbers around 30,000, many more people "play", or attend events, without formally joining. In the groups I observed in Meridies and Calontir, a solid 10–20% of event attendees were not members, (including myself and many of my friends in college.) though many of these non-members said they intended to eventually join when they became more established in the society or had more money. Membership is required for the individual to hold office and receive some of the honors by which one acquires status and rank within the Society, but not to attend most events. An independent minority of attendees who are actively reenacting non-members said they simply liked to hang out, without the need to participate in "any bureaucracy" and "play as they pleased" without commitment. Non-members usually are asked to pay a few dollars more to participate in events, and seem to be fully welcome as long as they do so. The general atmosphere is one of inclusion and welcome to all, and a special effort is made to welcome those who seem particularly shy or awkward.

The SCA is a not-for-profit educational organization of historical reenactors. The two distinct characteristics of the Society that make it a classic reenacting organization are both facets of time. First, it is the Society for Creative *Anachronism*. An **anachronism** is something out of time, and the SCA is a creative world of shared, interactive play and make-believe located in an idealized version of time. Everyone that falls within the genre time period reenacts together *at once, in the same "play" or reenactment time* despite the fact that their individual persona or impressions are from historical periods spread out over a millenium. It is agreed that a 5th century smith from Scotland, a 14th century knight from Germanic areas, a 10th century Viking, and a 16th century Tudor lady in waiting can interact in good humor. . . in a camp in the middle of Missouri. Anachronism, the out of time dimension, frees SCAdians to interact in a way not usually found in the very chronologically-aware Civil War or Revolutionary War groups. Second, the SCA period includes the time of the European Middle Ages up through the Renaissance. The SCA seeks out the practical history, arts, skills, and culture of pre-17th century Europe. So, a time and geographical period sets the boundaries of the SCA reenactment genre. Generally, you can get away with anything ranging from ~400–1700 CE (Common Era). The boundaries of time and geography are sometimes stretched, however. The original focus of the group was the European Medieval period, but you can find many individuals and groups dedicated to cultures and characters from the edges of that genre. Byzantine, Arabic, and a variety of Asian cultures are represented, though in much smaller numbers than mainstream European reenactors. Television series, movies, and novels can inspire surges in the popularity of particular cultures and time periods. Everything from *How to Train Your Dragon* to *Thor* movies and historical series to personal genealogy create affiliation for Vikings. Vikings are particularly popular in the Midwest and North central U.S. *The Tudors* created a huge surge in the popularity of Tudor and Elizabethan impressions. In the 1980s and '90s, the *Highlander* and *Outlander*

The Author, Kristina Hayen Hill, Catherine Chmidling at an SCA wedding. "Period" weddings are popular among SCA and Ren Faire reenactors.
Photo by Karol Chandler-Ezell

series were at the root of the huge abundance of Scottish impressions. The Romans are popular in some areas for a variety of reasons, including climate and the popularity of movies like *Gladiator*. I must say, after a brutal day of fieldwork in humid, 102-degree Kansas summer weather, I once gladly traded in my period-authentic yet very hot kilts for the light and cool Roman toga and sandals from a merchant. I changed my persona from Scottish to a late Roman herbalist with amused assistance from my key informants that afternoon. Since I had not yet created a permanent, long term persona, this was considered to be part of a natural experimental phase. As the temperature climbed, many others decided to "go Roman" just to get some relief from the heat. My friends that are active in the SCA have had some of their personae evolve over time. I've watched a surprising number experiment with different cultures as the time period catches their interest.

The SCA is a paraculture; and the goal of the society is to creatively develop and portray personae from the SCA period, using period-correct artifacts in a friendly *gentle* social environment. I say creative and gentle because everyone is expected to act and be treated as *gentlefolk* and everyone is to be tolerated and welcomed as long as they behave in this courteous manner. Gentle forms of address and chivalrous, courtly behavior are expected. Again and again, you hear SCAdians tell you, "this is the Middle Ages as they should have been," which means that everyone behaves in a courtly and chivalrous manner.

Maps of SCA distribution can be seen through links at the society's official website (www. sca.org). The Known World is organized into Kingdoms, with the densest membership and activity in the U.S., Canada, the U.K., Australia, and anywhere in the world U.S. military bases are located. This is because the SCA is very popular among university students and military personnel, especially the Navy and Air Force. If you look at maps of non-U.S. SCA groups, you can see that many of them center around U.S. military bases and universities. (See Table 5.1 for a list of SCA Kingdoms around the world, or look up SCA Geography on the SCA's official website www.sca.org for up-to-date information.) As membership waxes or wanes over time and

Table 5.1—*SCA Kingdoms around the world. Nations and continents are in bold, states and territories in regular font. To see the individual kingdom webpages, territories, and events, go to the Society for Creative Anachronism's homepage and check "SCA Geography." You can link directly to each kingdom or find where in The Known World you are.*

SCA Kingdom	Mundane Geographic Location
Aethelmearc	**U.S.:** central/western Pennsylvania, western New York, and West Virginia
An Tir	**U.S.:** Oregon, Washington, northern Idaho **Canada:** British Columbia, Yukon and Northwest Territories
Ansteorra	**U.S.:** Texas east of the Mountain time zone, Oklahoma
Artemisia	**U.S.:** Montana, most of Utah, western Wyoming and Colorado, southern Idaho
Atenveldt	**U.S.:** Arizona
Atlantia	**U.S.:** Maryland; District of Columbia; North Carolina; South Carolina; Virginia; Augusta, Georgia
Avacal	**Canada:** eastern British Columbia, Alberta, Saskatchewan
Caid	**U.S.:** southern California, Greater Las Vegas Area, Hawaii
Calontir	**U.S.:** Kansas, Missouri, Iowa, Nebraska, and northern Arkansas
Drachenwald	**Europe, Africa, Middle East, Sweden, Austria, Germany, Israel, Italy, Finland, Netherlands, France, Ireland, Spain, South Africa, United Kingdom, Greece**
Ealdormere	**Canada:** Ontario (except for Essex County, and Northwestern Ontario around Thunder Bay)
East	**U.S.:** Eastern New York, eastern Pennsylvania, New Jersey, Delaware, Massachusetts, Connecticut, Rhode Island, Vermont, New Hampshire, Maine **Canada:** Newfoundland, Nova Scotia, New Brunswick, Quebec
Gleann Abhann	**USA.:** Mississippi, Louisiana, most of Aransas, and Memphis, Tennessee
Lochac	**Australia, New Zealand, Antarctic**
Meridies	**U.S.:** Alabama, almost all of Georgia, a bit of Florida panhandle, most of Tennessee, pats of southern Kentucky
Middle	**U.S.:** Illinois, Indiana, part of Kentucky, Ohio, lower Michigan, Scott County in Iowa **Canada:** small part of Ontario
Northshield	**U.S.:** North Dakota, South Dakota, Minnesota, Wisconsin, upper peninsula of Michigan **Canada:** Manitoba and northwestern Ontario
Outlands	**U.S.:** New Mexico, most of Colorado, parts of Nebraska; Eastern Wyoming, El Paso & Hudspeth counties in Texas
Trimaris	**U.S.:** Florida (except western panhandle) Panama
West	**U.S.:** northern California, northern Nevada, Alaska, **ASIA:** Japan, Korea, Thailand, and Pacific Rim, **Far East:** Japan

social alliances within the SCA's various local groups shifts, the exact borders of the kingdoms sometimes shift, much as they did in the historic middle ages. New kingdoms arise, breaking away from the edges of older ones or forming when a large kingdom divides. From the time I first interacted with the very active SCA groups in central Arkansas as a teenager and when I was finishing up my dissertation fieldwork in Missouri, the kingdom of Meridies reorganized and Arkansas became part of the new kingdom of Gleann Abhann.

Within kingdoms, local and regional chapters are organized into households, ridings, colleges, cantons, marches, shires, baronies, principalities and a variety of other groupings. The groups are ranked by number of members. Households are the smallest grouping, consisting of several friends sharing similar interests and led by a Lord and Lady. Members of a household tend to work and play together more frequently than they do with other members in their area, though sometimes households are formed as a local group in the absence of a nearby larger grouping. Large towns, smaller cities and/or universities often support colleges, cantons, or shires. Shires consist of several individuals, including a few households and/or other societies and groups. Cities are usually necessary to support a barony, with the modern cities of Tucson, Kansas City, St. Louis, and Austin all supporting baronies. Access to frequent societal activities is important, and thus suburbs or nearby cities surrounding these baronies often support their own shires and other groupings. A smaller core group often forms the social center for members—a few to a few dozen individuals that reenactors see and engage in social activities with frequently.

Kingdoms are led by a king (usually) or queen and that person's consort. The Crown is won through prowess in combat during events called Crown Lists. The fighters in the kingdom compete in a tournament, with the winner becoming the Prince and heir apparent for a trial period (of 3-6 months) before ascending to the throne at Coronation. Though I use the male terms, females sometimes win. In that case, she becomes the Princess with her consort and then the Queen with her consort. You can easily find out who the current rulers and heirs are for each kingdom from their websites. Current rulers usually have profiles that members can read to learn more about their personae's preferences (and especially allergies or medical conditions) so that ritual gifts are not harmful or unpleasant. For instance, gifts of handcrafted wool might cause an allergic reaction in some; homebrewed mead would not be enjoyed by someone who does not drink alcohol; and pastries would be a painful gift for a diabetic. Besides, how else might you know that your new ruler shares your love of dragons? or bees? Kingdoms are not seated in a particular town but rather with the current rulers who take care to spend time throughout the kingdom during their reign. The duties of the crown are time-consuming, and often a court of friends and allies assist in the duties of royalty. Different kingdoms have evolved fairly different cultures with very different flavors. Overall rules for all groups in all kingdoms of the SCA abide by the Corpora, a set of rules and guidelines adopted by the Society. New members are encouraged to learn the appropriate rules and social structures from The Known World Handbook. When I first interacted, it was a photocopied, spiral bound booklet. It has been available online since the early days of the internet. A variety of newsletters that began as mailed photocopied versions in the 1970s and '80s have evolved into a variety of forms over the years into lovely websites and emagazines as well as Youtube channels. Most can be linked to directly from the SCA or kingdom websites.

Two gentlewomen relax in their finery. Great attention is given to detail in clothing accessories, and even activities. Ladies will often practice historically accurate crafts in a picturesque setting made of their period artifacts, activities, and even chatter make for a picturesque scene.
Copyright Jupiter Images.

The smaller groups are often arranged in a nested hierarchy, though not always. In other words, though a shire is smaller than a barony which is smaller than a kingdom; the shire usually reports directly to the king's court and is not nested underneath a barony. The organization is feudal, with ceremonial rankings by group, but this is very much a method of organizing and arranging social events based on member population. The individual members are treated with the type of respect and given the rights one would expect in an egalitarian society. Smaller group leadership and responsibilities are handled by people chosen through elections, appointment, or skills-based competition. In anthropological terms, status is achieved through display of skill and dedication although the old titles used are revived from feudal, ascribed-status cultures. SCA kings and other lords are given respect for both their individual prowess and their offices, and the individuals holding those places must win their right to their titles in competition.

To Play

So what do SCA reenactors do? Like the other types of reenactors discussed, they select a time period that appeals to them. The time period is rather broad in the SCA compared to Civil War or even Renaissance Faire reenactors. Though most choose Western European cultures as their focus, a variety of other options are available, including Asian, Mediterranean, and Near Eastern cultures as long as the time period rules are observed. They dress in clothing replicating the styles of the Middle Ages and Renaissance to socialize at a number of events including feasts, tournaments, wars, workshops, craft fairs, classes, and practices. While they are there, each portrays his or her "persona", *a fictional person set into a historically feasible narrative background*. In other words, they do not reenact actual historical figures. For instance, you cannot arrive at an SCA event and claim to be Henry VIII, one of his wives, or another particular person from history. By contrast, this is *exactly* what you *would* do at a historical Renaissance Festival or

Faire. The reason is that at a Renaissance Festival you are playing a role in a public performance, so you take on a character from a literary or historical figure from the time period being portrayed. By contrast, SCAdians are creating a new version of themselves with an identity that would be plausible in the time period they are researching and seeking to experience in a practical way. SCA personae are historically feasible. The background, skills, clothing, artifacts, heraldic device, and name should match. Many SCA reenactors try out several personae before settling on a favorite. This favorite "real" persona can then be registered, going through a thorough vetting by the College of Arms in the SCA who check the persona for consistency and historical feasibility and ensure that it does not duplicate another member's persona. The names and heraldic devices for each registered persona must pass muster with the College of Arms.

To begin, most people encounter the SCA in three ways: seeing reenactments; word of mouth; and finding them on the internet. First, they see SCA members out at play, either at a demonstration event or some sort of practice. Demonstration type events include reenacted demonstrations for the public such as fighting, dancing, music, archery, and crafts at local festivals, faires, and public events. Practices are also common ways for Mundanes (SCA folk call non-SCA either folk "mundanes" or "moderns" and refer to the non-SCA world as "the Mundane or Modern World") to encounter and observe SCA reenactors. Fighter practice is commonly held in public parks and on college campuses, drawing in a trickle of interested parties who are fascinated by the activity. Archery practice requires a safer environment (because of all the flying projectile weapons) but also draws in passersby. Dance and music practice or demonstrations bring in still another type of interested party. The SCA recruits new members in this way much the same as other reenacting groups do. They have individuals who are very charismatic and eager to talk with outsiders about what the SCA does. The recruiters typically talk to interested parties in great detail, hang out for a while, let them try their hand at a few reenacting crafts or skills, and then arrange to contact them for follow-up information. This contact person, often known as the group's *hospitalier* or *chatelain,* usually helps the new recruit to begin generating a persona and helps them borrow garb period-appropriate clothing for their first event. This is the same pattern Civil War reenactors use, and it seems to be quite a successful way to bring in interested parties.

The second major way of recruiting new reenactors is through word of mouth. A reenactor tells a friend or acquaintance about their reenacting and invites them along. Since SCAdians really enjoy what they do, they often want friends to come and give it a try. In this case, the friend is usually the facilitator, though they often get assistance from SCA friends with the process of enculturating a newby. Often reenactors cross genres, recruiting friends from other types of fandom. For instance, LARPers, cosplayers, or gamers might be recruited into the SCA by a friend who thinks they might like the SCA, too. SCAdians have long known to put up fliers or announcements at book stores, comic shops, and fan conventions.

A third way to recruit new reenactors is the internet. SCAdians may be interested in the practical arts and skills of the middle ages, but they are Renaissance men (and women) of the technology. The SCA had a presence on the internet as soon as there was an internet (and before through bulletin board systems.) In addition to the Society websites, there are Youtube channels, merchants, and private sites that will let you see anything from diaries from Wars (see below), demonstrations of crafts, and genre-themed art. Social media lets reenactors interact and maintain connections in between reenactments and serves to recruit as well.

So, how do you enculturate a new SCA reenactor? The willingness to come play is the first requirement. Playing the part is also important, and appearances matter. Often, someone will lend you clothing, called 'garb,' that is appropriate to the time period. Soon, though, you begin to make your own garb. One of the first and continuing activities that reenactors engage in is foraging for materials and patterns to construct good garb. In this great search for garb, the other details are passed on: How do you act? How do you address people of various ranks? What do all these new terms mean? What's an event? What's a war? And, based on the clothing styles you like, what time period and geographic location are you going to choose for your persona? These are the sorts of rich enculturating processes that take place alongside the act of making garb together. Throughout the reenacting cultures, acquiring garb and other gear is one of the most central activities through which reenactors socialize and bond.

The newby often gets a starter persona with the help of his or her friends. As they become acclimated and have a chance to learn to do their own research, new reenactors begin to settle on the details for a long-term persona. Discussing persona and the factors pro and con for particular historical periods and cultures is a major social activity in the SCA. Many people take a few years to develop their main persona, which becomes their identity in the reenacting community. (That said, they often enjoy playing at different personae when the mood strikes. As mentioned before, several SCAdians played Roman to beat the heat, and occasionally take a little persona vacation to try on a different character/period for a little variety.) SCA persona are different from Civil War and other battle/war-based reenactors in that the reenactors maintain a central, permanent persona. When referring to other reenactors, SCA reenactors use their SCA persona at most times. They also occasionally appear to have a mild form of personality disorder, as you'll hear them refer to their 'other self' in terms of their activities or history. This is important, for the SCA persona is both integrated into the reenactor and kept as an alter ego. The balancing of this reveals the function of this type of reenacting. The SCA persona is a personality over which the reenactor has control: it is a character whose name, history, background, talents, and personality can be created, edited, and refined over time. The reenactor owns it, and the persona can become real within SCA social settings once others recognize it, receiving awards and achieving social status. The persona is also *you as you would make yourself*, a self that you incorporate into a new you as you create it. This alter ego, which exists in the shared society, is a key trait of paracultures.

Think about the implications, particularly if you are frustrated or unhappy with your life and social environment as it is. With an alternate persona, you can visit another time and place as a person you enjoy being, in the company of others who are doing the same thing. This is why SCA reenactors call what they do "play." It is make-believe, and it is cooperative play that is socially constructed. The others agree to play by the rules, making the SCA, or "Known World", a place you can visit in company with your friends as the person you want to be. Far from being psychologically unhealthy, this allows a much-needed break from every life's stresses and pressures. Some people choose to escape in this way from lives that are unhappy, unsuccessful or otherwise unpleasant, others from lives that are happy or successful, yet full of pressure. When this happens, you often see inversion of status. For instance, people who have high-status daily (Mundane) lives often crave a persona which has a more leisurely pace of life. Surgeons, engineers, and a variety of other professionals often choose to portray simple "tavern wenches", smiths, or peasants. By contrast, reenactors with low status in the Mundane world often crave and con gain recognition and high status within the reenacting society. The role reversal is part of the therapeutic nature of the escapism.

What else is involved in entering the reenacting world? The new reenactor learns behaviors such as bowing, speaking gently, and using honorific terms for others. Jargon, slang, or specialized language for both one's time period and for the shared society of the SCA is learned. Garb, device, persona, and mundane are just the beginning. The proper forms of polite address for people of various positions is learned, though milady and milord (forms of "my lady" and "my lord". When capitalized "Lord" and "Lady" refer only to individuals who have earned an Award of Arms—a formal title. My Lady and My Lord) are good when the rank of the individual is unknown. In general, it is impossible to be too polite. Taboos and customs must be learned. For instance, the royal presence (the area around the King and Queen, Prince and Princess) is not an area one strolls across casually. Proper obeisance and respect must be shown. The archery and fighting fields are also sacrosanct for safety reasons. Children and new reenactors are taught immediately not to enter an area where fighting or weapons could be in play. This is particularly important, given that the archers use real bows and arrows that could be deadly even with blunted practice points. Heavily armored fighters often have impaired peripheral vision with their helms on, and though they use safety swords instead of raw metal blades, they could harm an unarmored, unpadded person. Though regalia and gear sometimes includes real knives, it is taboo to draw a blade without calling out a loud "clear", and it is definitely taboo to threaten someone, even in play. Many events actually require that such blades be safely tied or secured so that they won't accidentally fall out or come lose. Rude or unchivalrous behavior is verboten and can result in social censure and even a request that the individual leave.

The Characters and Events

Where to start? There are many groups of interest within SCA reenacting. Fighters are probably the most noticeable. Men and women who are fighters must learn from a more experienced member how to safely participate in their chosen style of combat. While jousting and horseback fighting do occur, they are comparatively rare in the SCA. Horses are expensive, and fighting on horseback is very dangerous, even with blunted weapons. You are much more likely to see jousting and medieval combat on horseback at a Renaissance Faire, done by professionals. Most SCA fighters are 'sword' fighters on foot. I put sword in quotations because they actually tend to use boffer or boffle swords made of metal cores encased in foam pool noodle and wrapped in tape. These round swords do not cut, but deliver ample blunt force. Fighters are required to wear minimum safety gear, including a padded helm. Armor varies from padded leather to chain mail to plate metal breastplates and can be quite expensive. Fighter practice is often held weekly or biweekly, making it an easy activity to go observe. Non-fighters often go to fighter practice to watch the fighters and hang out, chatting with other reenactors. It is common to see several ladies embroidering or sewing on the sidelines, chatting with other reenactors during fighter practice. This provides a routine, frequent activity for socializing. Archery practice is similar to fighter practice, though archers and fighters are often different crowds. Archers participate in battles using blunted arrows for safety but use "real" arrows in safe shooting ranges. Knife or ax-throwing, quarterstaffs, maces, and a variety of other weapons are available as well as a variety of different types of swords.

Though fighters in their armor often get screentime because. . . well, fully armored combat is photogenic. The SCA is about practical arts and skills of the past, though, and that includes more than just the arts and skills of war. Arts and Crafts people include several groups. Weavers and fabric makers often enjoy each other's company and have events and activities together. Skills range from embroidery, sewing, knitting, leatherworking, ceramics, smithing, jewelry-making, cooking, soapmaking, herbalism, brewing, calligraphy, and more. Most reenactors participate in several different Arts and Crafts skills as a part of learning more and enriching the reenacting experience. A great deal of appreciation and recognition amongst reenactors is shown for effort and/or excellence in crafts. Arts and Crafts includes lectures and workshops on historical topics, from eating customs of the Celts to period-appropriate underwear. A huge part of the social interaction between reenactors is exchange of information and historical sources. Facebook feeds and newsletters are full of links to historical articles, museums, research, and how-to instructions. Social media interactions include progress reports on sewing projects, armor, artifact reconstructions, and more. Events are still very important, because the SCA is at its heart still live reenactment, but social media and internet resources let the reenactment community have access to a larger, broader reenacting world that interacts with other genres, fandoms, and interest groups. Ongoing learning is very much a part of the historical and researching emphasis of reenactors.

Awards and social rank within the Society are given for excellence in Arts and Crafts. For example, an Award of Arms, and the right to be a Lord as Lady, Dancers and Musicians have practices and events and are recognized in much the same way. Though there are people who specialize or excel in these areas, all SCA reenactors are welcome to participate in these activities and most do to some extent.

Though demonstration events are held in the public eye, most SCA activities are private, focused on social activities for the reenactors with minimal intrusion from the Mundane world. Language, behavior, and dress are kept period when possible to emphasize that this is reenacting, not a Mundane activity. In this way, SCA activities are quite different from Renaissance Faires and many of the events of Civil War and other war reenactors. It is private, with the emphasis on shared play in a safe social environment, not a public exhibition. The shared alternate reality is best enjoyed when it is not spoiled by the mundane world. It is sacred time—a chance to escape normal societal roles. (see Chapter 8)

Officers for the local groups have business meetings, which are often social as well. While business is handled, members enjoy period food, crafts, watching films, and the sharing of information. Meetings to work on garb or artifacts as a group are also common activities.

The leaders of a given group hold 'court', an activity in which the reenactors assemble and go over society business in a formal atmosphere. Schedules and announcements are made, awards are given, and individuals are recognized for their skill and/or work. Afterwards, there are often celebratory activities like music, dancing, and feasting. Reenactors often wear their best and most elaborate garb to court, as this is a formal environment for showing off one's finery.

Feasts are jolly events in which some of the reenactors prepare elaborate, period-authentic meals for the delight of the reenacting community. Reenactors from surrounding areas will often attend another group's feast, giving them an opportunity to socialize with each other. Participants are expected to bring their own feast gear (cutlery, plate, bowl, cup or tankard) as well as any elaborate beverages. Water and lemonade are often provided as part of the feast, with guests bringing mead, beer, ale, or other beverages of their choice if site appropriate and subject to local mundane liquor laws. While appreciation of period-appropriate alcohol is a favorite adult pastime, great care is taken to make sure that minors do not drink alcohol at SCA-sponsored events. Indeed, though there are very adult activities in the later hours, great care is taken to keep any event with children present very family-friendly. Children's activities are often part of most events.

Events include a variety of activities and are usually hosted by a local group with anyone invited. Battles, arts and crafts competitions or exhibitions, merchant faires, dances, archery competitions, and wars are common types of events. Several activities are often combined for an event. Most will include a feast in the evening, and at least some arts and crafts activities or educational activities are included in an event to make sure that everyone is able to entertain themselves. Fighting is one of the most popular activities, both to participate in and to observe.

Wars are some of the most spectacular events. Many last for one to two weeks, with the average being a Friday through the following Sunday. Reenactors will take vacation time to come out and experience this prolonged immersion experience. Wars are held in a secluded place, with an attempt to minimize Mundane intrusion. Multiple kingdoms participate, and they can get quite large. The largest and best known is the annual Pennsic War hosted in Pennsylvania by the Kingdom of Aethelmearc in late July–August with over 10,000 attendees and 200 merchants. (see www.pennsicwar.org or go to YouTube to see a plethora of video and photos from Pennsic). The Estrella War hosted by Atenveldt (Arizona) in February, the Gulf Wars hosted by Kingdom Meridies in March, the Lilies War hosted by Calontir near Kansas City in June, and

A *child kneels at Court to receive a commendation on a task well done. Much effort is made to encourage learning, skills, and chivalrous behavior, especially in children.*
Photo by Kristina Hayen.

the Great Western War in Caid in October are the big interkingdom wars. Wars involve hundreds or thousands of reenactors simultaneously and offer a much deeper reenacting experience than shorter-term events. Battles during wars are the closest SCAdians come to the large Battle reenactments favored by war reenactors.

Period weddings are another type of event thrown by individuals. Many reenactors enjoy the pomp and ceremony of the Middle Ages more than modern wedding trappings and elect to have Medieval or Renaissance Weddings. Often, most of the guests will also dress in period garb. SCAdian wedding clothing may include elaborate, often handmade medieval or Elizabethan creations covered in hand-bending, embroidery, and lace—and that's just the males! Period wedding garb is worthy of many museum exhibits with attention given to ensuring historically accurate style and fabric.

SCA Environment

The SCA social environment is different for different stages of life. It is family friendly, with an emphasis on providing a fun, safe, and educational environment for all ages. Many families reenact together, and there are special events for children. If they don't start from a reenacting family, high school is a common age for people to enter reenacting. Great care is taken to reassure their anxious parents that they will be safely and attentively cared for while they are at events.

College-aged reenactors are allowed more freedoms and able to participate in more risky or at least risqué behavior, though alcohol use is discouraged and actively prevented when possible for anyone underage. Adults from young to old find social groups with which to share a variety of interests, though most SCA reenactors I have observed are under sixty. As I've had opportunities to interact with the SCA at different stages of my life, I've observed that it is both the same world and a different world for reenactors at different stages of life with reenactors finding social groups that share their interests.

Fieldwork Experience

Most of my initial fieldwork was in Calontir, though it built upon my experiences from high school and undergraduate college in the Kingdom of Meridies (Now Gleann Abhann). My informants were mostly members of Meridies and Calontir, though some belonged to other kingdoms. Since the first edition of this book was written, I have done additional fieldwork in Ansteorra and continue my contacts with reenactors I befriended in other kingdoms. I keep up observation of the SCA through their publications and social media.

While in most contexts my interaction with SCA society was either informal or in the form of semi-structured interviews, I was able to conduct observation and participant observation as well. Unlike a place of business or even events designed to demonstrate to a regular audience, SCA events stress the need for everyone to "remain period" by dressing, speaking, and behaving in the agreed-upon form of "the modern middle ages." The boundary line between the performers and audience is not present, since everyone is participating in the same activity—group play. Since these events exist in a discrete time period and location, however, the researcher can "go there" and stay in the participant observation mode for a prolonged period of up to 10 days. This was a valuable way to establish rapport that is much more like standard anthropological fieldwork methods than other contexts.

During my fieldwork, I attended community activities and helped with tasks like food preparation, "riding the tents" during a thunderstorm, and dying cloth. I also attended ritual performances like "court"and "battles" as well as the classes on medieval and SCA-related topics that are at the core of this reenactment-oriented community.

Over the course of the participant observation, I performed and experienced the activities that all "new" SCA members must complete. These included selecting a persona, creating a history and background for this persona, and then creating an appropriate wardrobe of "garb". I obtained assistance from a few key consultants with these tasks and they were gracious enough to invite me to several events, on shopping expeditions, and even into their homes to work

Details from medieval and Renaissance art are used as inspiration for reenacted rituals and artifacts.
Copyright Jupiter Images.

together on my persona. The extensive literature research and labor involved in creating the various physical and nonphysical aspects of a persona are considered to be one of the most

Court proceedings in the Kingdom of Calontir. The ritualized nature of court allows SCAdians to enjoy the shared acting out of medieval ideals and forms.
Photo by Kristina Hayen.

central and pleasurable aspects of this community. One of the fun things about interacting with SCAdians through media is maintaining those connections and the fun of engaging in the historical curiosity and research that is a part of it. Several fandoms overlap with reenacting genres, so several of us are linked through multiple interest groups.

Most members trade services and skills in a sort of generalized or balanced reciprocity. I traded herbal information sources, recipes and preparations as my way of contributing to the group and reciprocating for the assistance and gifts offered to me by other members of the community. At the Lilies War, a 10-day event near Kansas City, I was identified (by my key consultants) as an expert and contributed by volunteering to teach a class. My class drew many individuals who were interested in herbal remedies, and in this way I was able to obtain volunteers for interviews. In order to avoid "polluting" my sample on herbal use, I taught a class on Mineral Herbalism. During this class I gave a history of Mineral Herbalism and showed my students how to make salt and clay-based products instead of herbal remedies.

Later, several of the students from this class and their friends offered their encampment for trying the preparations, and to reciprocated by giving interviews. At prolonged SCA events, groups of friends or members of organizational groups such as households, shires, and baronies set up their pavilions near each other to form camps. I arrived at their camp with my interview materials and a variety of mineral preparations demonstrated in class. I had noticed several common ailments during the course of the war, so I briefly left the camp to go to a nearby store to purchase supplies for larger quantities of salts, oatmeal, and other supplies to make remedies for the ladies. Everyone had sore feet from walking long distances, often in thin slippers or uncomfortable period shoes on uneven ground. The ladies' costumes revealed large expanses of shoulders and bosom that had painfully sunburned, and all were suffering from sunburned faces from being outdoors all day every day. In addition, several days without warm water in the campground showers and camping "in period style" while sweating in the heat of a Missouri/Kansas summer *while wearing full medieval costumes* had left many ladies with unfortunate skin conditions such as heat rash and acne. In my class, I had demonstrated cooling foot baths (with salt that would dissolve in cold water), facial masks, acne and blister plasters, and plasters for treating sunburn with my audience in mind. So, for this visit, I brought additional quantities so that everyone could enjoy sampling the remedies.

When I arrived at the camp, I discovered that the ladies had ordered 'their lords' (their husbands) to haul nearly 40 gallons of water over half a mile (uphill) and to set up an appropriate setting. This paraculturally—appropriate setting of open pavilions with pillows, stools, and chairs scattered on the ground for us to sit upon as well as rugs so we could walk barefoot—a luxury in the camp. The ladies relaxed, chatted, and took turns being interviewed while they enjoyed foot baths, facials, and sunburn treatments. Everyone had brought something to contribute, from pots of honey (for snacks and to add into mud masks) and homemade mead to a bard with a great harp to play music for us. The men even fanned us while doing the hard work of attempting to heat the large pots of water at the campsite for facial steams and warm foot baths.

In addition to the ladies' party, I interviewed a key consultant in a public place near the classroom, then gave her a gift of perfume. She then showed off her perfume, and all of her friends wanted some. I offered consultants their selection from a basket of homemade preparations as a thank you for then valuable time. In this setting/subculture, a homemade or herbal item can be more enticing than a cash reward for interviews. Most members of the community have sufficient income to participate in an expensive hobby (garb, paraphernalia, events are costly). What they crave is specialized knowledge of the culture with which they seek to connect. Herbal consumers wanted information from an expert. Practitioners appreciate shared knowledge as a sign of respect and evaluated my information as a judgment of my expertise. Sharing recipes and remedies was a way to make a place for myself within their society in a respectful way while contributing appreciated information. I was careful not to sell any of the remedies and so not compete with herbalists at the events who were attempting to sell remedies as part of their businesses.

I began this fieldwork searching for herbal practitioners, but what I discovered about reenactors and the differences among the different types of reenactors convinced me that there was a need for ethnographic research among SCA society. It was the realization of the importance of personae, alternate shared realities, and the sacred time in reenacting in the SCA which revealed how very adaptive a strategy reenacting is for modern Americans.

Assignments

I. Learning More About the Society for Creative Anachronism

Assignment A: Basic Information

1. What is the SCA currently? _____

_____

_____

2. Approximately how many official members does the SCA have? _____

3. How many kingdoms are there? _____ and what is their geographic range?

_____

_____

4. What does **anachronism** mean, and why is it an important part of SCA culture?

_____

_____

_____

5. What time period do SCAdians reenact? _____

6. What geographic/cultural area do SCAdians reenact? _____

_____

7. What is a mundane? _____

8. What is a persona? _____

9. What is garb? _____

10. What are "wars"? _____

Name _____ Date _____

Assignment B: Researching the SCA Online

Go to the Society for Creative Anachronism homepage at http://www.sca.org to gather more information about the SCA around the world and in your area.

Get to Know the SCA:

Search for information pages and events calendars to find out more about the SCA. There are pages/tabs specifically designed to help newcomers find out more about how to join or become involved.

1. What sorts of activities are available to SCA members?

_____

_____

_____

2. How is participation in these activities an important part of engaging in reenactor paraculture?

_____

_____

_____

3. How is this similar to the ethnographic methods and goals of participant observation?

_____

_____

_____

4. What behaviors and practices are emphasized in SCAdian culture?

_____

_____

_____

5. What linguistic differences do you notice between everyday speech and writing and the script on the SCA webpages?

_____

_____

_____

6. What is the difference between a lady and a Lady? (and a lord and a Lord)?

_____

_____

_____

Getting to Know Your Local SCA:

1. In what kingdom do *you* live? _____

2. What is your kingdom's website? _____

3. What smaller SCA group is in the SFA area? _____

4. How and when is your local kingdom's "king" chosen? _____

_____

_____

5. Who are the current rulers of your kingdom, and what are their personae like?

_____

_____

_____

6. Where can you meet/see some SCAdians face to face in your area? Look at the local events calendar or contact information to see what activities and locations are good options. List at least 2.

Location?   Activity?   Time?

_____   _____   _____

_____   _____   _____

_____   _____   _____

II. Understanding & Interpreting SCA Involvement

1. How does one acquire status in SCA society? Give several options.

_____

_____

_____

2. How do SCAdians attempt to achieve the period rush where they become their persona?

_____

_____

_____

3. Are SCAdians more privately-oriented or publically-oriented in their activities?

_____

_____

_____

4. How is the SCAdian persona different from other reenactors' impressions?

_____

_____

_____

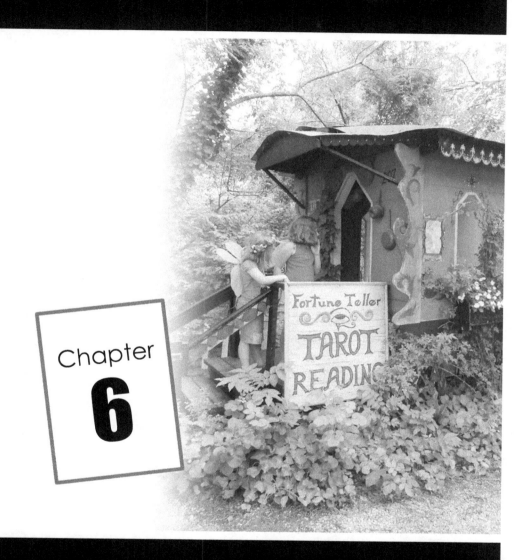

Chapter **6**

Renaissance Faires and Festivals

Introduction

Renaissance Faires are public festivals with a Renaissance Europe theme. Even though the European Renaissance started in Italy and lasted from the 14th-17th centuries throughout Europe, most American and Canadian "Ren Faires" are set in Elizabethan or Tudor England..with a touch of Robin Hood and his Merry men and fairies mixed in for good, anachronistic measure. So, the stated time period and genre of characters and artifacts is usually focused on the Tudor through Elizabethan periods (1500s–1600s C.E.). with an emphasis on King Henry VIII and Queen Elizabeth of England. Usually called Ren Faires or simply Faires, these festivals are a mix of craft fair; theatrical or skill performances; and of course, historical reenactment. Faires are distinct from other forms of reenacting activities in that they are innately commercial ventures. While both SCA and Civil War reenactors put on some public events, they both focus the core of their social activities around private, all-reenactor events designed to exclude non-reenactors so as to have a more "pure" reenacting experience. Faires are designed to engage the public, with hired actors, performers, and Faire workers alongside merchants running businesses. The public are customers, paying an admission fee and enjoying the Faire as a recreational destination similar to a theme park. The atmosphere is created by the various Faire employees and set design, letting the visitor arrive with less necessary preparation. While visitors are encouraged to dress in a Renaissance style to better enjoy the experience, it

Brant Johnson and Miranda Witherspoon at Texas Renaissance Festival, in character. Notice the horns and pointed ears—part of a fantasy persona.
Photo by the Witherspoon Family.

is not demanded or even expected that most will do so. Instead, customers are necessary for these commercial ventures to be successful, with their money spent allowing the reenactors their chance to reenact. Among the commercial activities, there are still the reenactors—people who come to enact their Faire impression—to enjoy the fantasy of an alternate persona in the festival atmosphere. Some are consumers, some workers, some the merchants. They not only manage, but seem to better achieve their "period rush," or immersion into their persona, in the festival atmosphere filled with observers and non-reenactors. It is performance reenacting as well as living history exhibit.

Individual Faires vary in how historically authentic and narrowly they limit the festival's time period. Some Faires, or at least some reenactors and/or performers at the Faires take historical reconstruction very seriously. Korol-Evans (2009) in her *Renaissance Festivals: Merrying the Past and Present*, focused on the meticulous authenticity of performers at the Maryland Renaissance Festival. Herself both a reenactor and a scholar, Korol-Evans presents an ethnography of performers and how they interact with history, their roles, and the audience to create an interactive experience with history. Renaissance Faire and Festival reenactors perform and bring in the audience to the shared alternate reality. Being able to entertain and engage the (non-reenactor) audience enriches the sense of sacred time and immersion in the character. Even when they work for the Faire, the historical reenactors at Renaissance Festivals and Faires are still doing more than just an acting job. They are re-enacting, re-creating, and co-modifying the time period with their peers and audience. The festival is the ritual that lets them achieve this.

That being said, not everyone at the Renaissance Faire is concerned with historical authenticity. For many of the customers and attendees, it's just a day of entertainment with added flavor from their favorite historical or fictional genres. For many participants who dress up, it is an opportunity to show off fantastic costumes and play. Still others may be much more attached to fantasy reenactment. The unique property of Renaissance Festivals as compared to other types of historical reenactment is that all are welcome as long as they play nicely. In other words, the most meticulously correct living historian or Elizabethan performer is perfectly genial and welcoming to the cosplayer dressed as an anime character, the little girls in a Disney princess dress, a scary fairy, and an elf from one of Tolkien's novels. . . . as long as they play by the rules.

Old Festivals and Faires as Public Ritual

Faires are similar to old local festivals in Europe dating back to at least the Middle Ages. These local festivals were often based upon important events like weddings, coronations, harvest, holidays, or other happy events. Traveling performers and merchants came together for these events. Locals prepared festival foods, often showcasing the bounty of a harvest or local and/or seasonal delicacies. People could show off their skills and accomplishments, competing for prices and recognition. These festivals or faires drew in a great number of people from the area, making them opportunities for socialization, courtship, and showing off one's finery. In short, faires were happy events full of revelry, eating great food, commerce, spectators, and fun clothes. With the Renaissance, the social atmosphere in Europe was much happier and open than it had been in the Dark Ages. Historical accounts record these events as happy, exciting times. Many of these festivals became annual events and continue as part of local European traditions to this day. Mardi Gras, Carnival, May Day, Harvest festivals, and numerous other festivals are descended from these events.

Europeans also have "Renaissance Festivals," though they tend to focus on reenactment of local historical events. Websites like Renlist (www.therenlist.com/fairs) and Renfaire keep updated postings of North American, European, and Australian Renaissance Faires.

Seasonal or annual folk festivals and gatherings are common to many societies and serve the same function. Tailgating and homecoming festivities are good examples of modern behavior that are very much like these old festivals. There are public rituals like parades and reenactments, pep rallies, and chants or cheers designed to bring good luck to the teams. People dress in special clothes, decorations, and even costumes or face paint that they would not wear everyday. Special foods and drinks are prepared and shared, and there is a party atmosphere created. All of these festivals share a common trait: they all use special rituals that create a festival atmosphere for the participants.

Ritual and Sacred Time

The festival atmosphere creates an experience that anthropologists call *sacred time*. Watching and participating in public rituals like performances, parades, music, and acting out special roles creates this special shared social reality. When the various public rituals are enacted, and the festival itself is an atmosphere where participants are in a liminal state much of the time, people enjoy something called the liminal state. The festival atmosphere is one where the participants are freed from every-day social rules and inhibitions. The "betwixt and between" state of liminality Turner describes in his classic works on ritual are large-scale at festivals—but instead of progressing between life stages or ranks, that Turner described in his writings on sacred rituals, the festival participants are just engaging in a therapeutic escape from their everyday life and social environment. This is often emphasized by dramatic or outrageous costumes; masks; pranks; binging on food, alcohol, or other mind-altering substances; and other mischievous behavior not considered acceptable in everyday life. Often, **role reversal** is observed where people who normally have very low status are elevated while those with high status take on lower ranked roles. For instance, beggars, peasants, or other low-status individuals often become elevated to festival royalty. Today's Carnival Kings and beauty pageants at festivals are vestiges of this tradition. The May King and May Queen tradition observed in Great Britain is an example of local non-nobility being elevated to ritual royalty during a festival. Luckily, today's festival royalty don't face the risk of human sacrifice as they are reputed to have done in festivals from Europe's Celtic past. By contrast, high status individuals or fine upstanding citizens often dress as fools or clowns and run about flouting social rules. The escape provided by the sacred time of a festival is therapeutic to both the individuals who participate and the community at large, allowing frustrations and social pressures to be released in a ritualized way. This feel of freedom and escapism from normal social roles is what is captured by today's Renaissance Faires.

Origins of Modern Ren Faires

The oldest Ren Faires in the United States date to 1963. Phyllis Patterson and the Living History Center in California are credited with the idea of modern Renaissance Pleasure Faires. The Living History Center, a non-profit organization, maintained a 1580s-era English village as a reenactment event designed to entertain and educate. The Renaissance Pleasure Faires started in San Bernadino and Novato, California in the Spring and Fall every year. These Faires sold food, beer and other period alcohol, crafts, and Tudor-Elizabethan reproductions while entertaining with actors and stage shows, and the LHC made an attempt to keep the actors and performances as historically-accurate as possible. The old LHC faires were purchased by the Renaissance Entertainment Corporation in 1993. REC began a professional joust group and reorganized the Faires to a mixed response among faire workers and reenactors. These Renaissance Pleasure Faires continue today.

Renaissance Faires in the U.S

Today there are a few hundred Faires in the U.S. and Canada of various sizes. Some are small events that last a single weekend, while others run for a few months. The customers they draw vary from a few hundred to thousands annually. Faires may draw hundreds of thousands in larger cities. The Original Renaissance Pleasure Faire, now in Irwindale, California, draws over 200,000 guests per year. The Minnesota Renaissance Festival is advertised as the largest Renaissance Festival in the US, boasting an annual attendance of 300,000 people as of 2016. The Texas Renaissance Festival northwest of Houston claims 500,000 guests per year. The larger faires each employ a few thousand actors, performers, and others every year, many of them reenactors. Hundreds more craftsmen, artists, and other merchants participate at each. The sheer size of these faires and the many others demonstrate their popularity.

The most popular theme for Renaissance Festivals and Faires in the US are Elizabethan and Tudor England. A close third is Robin Hood. General Renaissance, medieval, and fantasy themes are also popular, though all of these elements appear at all of the Renaissance Faires, thanks to their inclusiveness and the fact that many of the same performers, merchants, and participants attend multiple fairs, bringing their favorite themes with them. Though each fair has an overall theme, most offer themed weekends to make the faire exciting and encourage people to attend multiple times. Most faires last between four to ten weekends, with some also hosting a few shorter events during other parts of the year.

Most weekends have a special theme such as Pirates, Highland Scottish, Irish/Celtic, Barbarians, Robin Hood, German/Oktoberfest, and Fantasy. Most autumn Renaissance Festivals have an Oktoberfest, and some that are spring festivals often have a special themed Oktoberfest weekend on the site. As someone who has been watching Renaissance Faires for a few decades now, there are trends from popular culture. Pirates remain very popular despite not being quite the right time period, but Romans and Robin Hood have declined in popularity. Faeries and elves remain popular, but other fantasy themed weekends have started explicitly advertising "Time Travelers' Weekend," "Once Upon A Time," and "Heroes and Villains" themes that invite fairy tales, science fiction, books, and movies. Special mention of "Warlocks and Witches" (Harry Potter being trademarked)," comic book heroes, Steampunk, Star Wars, and Dr. Who are intended to recruit fandoms and cosplayers from non-Renaissance fantasy genres. There is a distinct crossover element between different reenactment and cosplay groups. Some Faires even host gaming events for LARPers, Magic the Gathering, and other games.

Though Faires are advertised locally, it's quite easy to find Faires across the country using the internet and such sites as www.renfaire.com, www.Renaissance-Faire.com, and many more easily accessed with a search engine. These same sites offer information about Faire culture, merchandise, and entertainment. Many have advertisements for a multitude of merchants selling faire-themed books, costumes, arts, crafts, music, and accessories.

While the Faires are commercial ventures, they also seek to share reenactment and a taste of living history with the public. Even though many of the merchants, artisans, performers, and administrators do make a salary (or at least recoup costs for their hobby); they do it for love of the genre and experience. The reenacting experience of Faire folk just happens to be different in nature from many other types of reenactors. Faires are about performances, and in this way are similar to the living history demonstrations that other types of reenactors put on for public consumption. Faires are made up of a mixture of "true" reenactors and extras hired to just do the job. Most Faires do attempt to instill a true reenacting mentality and introduction to Rennie culture in any hired performers, however, as this improves the "feel" of the Faire.

One of the most telling ways to contrast Ren Faire and the seemingly-similar SCA experiences comes from my informants who had participated in both. SCA reenactors like to go to Ren Faires and even sometimes participate as demonstrators or organizers. I've been to a few Faires that were thrown by SCA groups. They were very short and small affairs lasting just one to two days, but many of the reenactors dressed and acted differently because they were attempting to replicate a Faire environment. Mostly, SCA reenactors participate in Ren Faires that others organize. Many of them stand out, as they refuse to surrender their period authenticity even for a brief Faire experience and come as their medieval personae. (Which is NOT Elizabethan or Tudor English and therefore not the correct Faire period). A few of my Faire consultants called these SCAs (pronounced Skah's) or SCAdians gloomy gusses and sighed over their refusal to "just have fun, it's a *Faire!*" It is interesting that SCA reenactors often call their reenacting experience play, yet have trouble exchanging their serious and authentic shared fantasy for the very public and openly fantastic play of the Faires. This is not true of all SCA reenactors, however. Many of them go to the Faire to "let my hair down and not worry about details!" A few of my consultants enjoyed dressing in their wilder garb, indulging in pirate, wizard, swashbuckler, or

A family tradition of Ren Faire participation. Billy Cordova, Miranda Witherspoon, and Dr. Elizabeth Witherspoon at the Texas Renaissance Festival, 2006.
Photo by the Witherspoon Family.

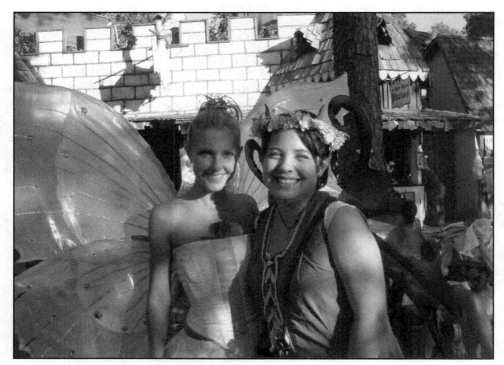

Kristi Jones (left) and Miranda Witherspoon dressed as faeries at a Ren Faire wedding in Texas. Renaissance Faire weddings are very popular, and may be very historically accurate, or very fantastically fanciful to suit the couple's preferences.
Photo by the Witherspoon Family.

faerie princess *costumes* (their change of use, not mine) that they knew would be too flashy or ill-received at SCA events. In many ways, they treat the Faires much as authentic people across history have—as a time of inversion and play.

A pair of my SCA consultants who wanted a period wedding without all of the fuss of having to 'make everything from scratch, just right' for an SCA wedding actually took the shortcut and had their wedding at the Kansas City Renaissance Festival. Their garb was period appropriate for their SCA personae, as were many of their close friends. They found the Ren Faire to be a useful compromise, however, because their non-reenacting family members were able to simply rent costumes from the Ren Faire. They had their period experience wedding with all of the details they wanted in decorations, music (Elizabethan lutes, flutes, and harps, of course), setting (a delightful reproduction Tudor chapel), and food (Ale, mead, turkey drumsticks, and a castle-shaped cake). The guests and family were "almost there on the time period" thanks to the assistance of the Faire's events office. The minister even dressed as an Elizabethan priest, and the parents of the groom and bride were able to let the event coordinator at the Faire fit them with elegant costumes for a very low rental cost. The event was fun for all, since guests received a free pass to the Faire to enjoy and "de-stress" all day. All in all, the festive atmosphere of the Faire let the newly formed extended family play at the Faire all day instead of focusing on the wedding details. They were very satisfied with their experience, and the guests had a delightful time. According to the Faire's event coordinator, Ren Faire weddings are very popular, and multiple weddings are often scheduled for each day of the Faire. Most Ren Faire offices have coordinators dedicated to weddings, and times may be booked more than a year in advance. There are even popular books and websites devoted to in Faire weddings.

Now that we have discussed what Faires are not, it seems appropriate to describe the events themselves. Most of my consultants were merchants at the Faires, selling herbal remedies or magical items. Some of them participated in both Faires and SCA, but most Faire folk preferred the Faire. Their stated reasons were that they could reasonably expect to make a living, they preferred the festive atmosphere, and they liked the magical quality of Faires more. Being commercial ventures, Faires do draw people who are coming to an entertainment and cultural destination. The Faires are ephemeral—only lasting a short time, so those who love them often stock up or binge on Faire merchandise to "get them through the year", as a few of my consultants explained. The merchandise includes short-lived items like food, face painting, and flower wreaths. Other popular items are jewelry, accessories, artwork, crafts, and toiletries that can be enjoyed for a long time, reminding visitors of their fun. A great deal of costumes are sold, however, that are really only wearable for Faires and Halloween. Caught up in the excitement of the Faire, many customers buy costumes and put it on immediately so they can join into the reenacting experience instead of feeling separated by their obviously everyday, non-Faire appearance.

People who have enjoyed the Faires once often plan and prepare for their next visit by dressing in costumes. Some go into detail as elaborate, if not as historically accurate, as the garb SCA reenactors wear. Many Faires encourage a very historically authentic setting from their employees, though many do not. So, at most Faires the visitor will see a mixture including a few people in garb that would impress even a Stitch Counter with a multitude of polyester-satin enrobed princesses and gossamer faeries. Faeries, pirates, and wenches are very popular at Faires. Girls from toddler to middle age seem to enjoy wearing gauze fairy wings and wreaths in their hair. Boys and men alike seem to enjoy swaggering like pirates, though the small boys seem to indulge with plastic cutlasses more often while the men appreciate the bosom-exposing fashions of the ladies.

Some Faires are held in tent cities while others have a variety of permanent structures in the Tudor or Elizabethan style. Many merchants have exciting setups such as tinkers' or gypsies' wagons to display their wares. There are multiple stages or entertainment areas. Some are small theaters where actors recreate Shakespeare-style plays or comedies. Moving through the crowds or on small performance areas, performers entertain with skits, improvisation, comedy, juggling, dancing, fire-eating, sword-swallowing, singing, music, and magic routines. Workers dressed and speaking in BFA (basic faire accent) man information booths and food vending. Basic Faire Accent is an accepted Elizabethan period grammatical style used for most Ren Faires & many theatrical groups, and pronunciation, costuming, and acting are practiced by employees at the Faire, and the Faire administration often give their employees classes before the Faire begins.

The Faire structures are made of wood, stone, thatch, and stucco—or at least replicas of these period materials. The décor is as medieval as possible as well, with banners and ribbons fluttering in breezes heavy with the smells of food and sounds of music. There is an attempt to give Faires a fairytale village look and feel. Trees provide dappled shade and make up secluded little grottoes designed to take visitors away from an industrial, concrete world. Paths are dirt or wooden to get away from standard concrete. The décor is a wild mix of colors, images, and items for sale, but an effort is made to at least try for Elizabethan or Tudor style. The music includes period instruments as well as entertainers singing, performing skits, or hawking their wares in Basic Faire Accent—the standard stage accent/Tudor accent adopted at the first American Faires. Employees of the Faires or acts hired to perform focus on fun and festive entertainment. Bawdy jokes or flirtation by Tudor-dressed and—speaking actors give visitors interaction. Numerous stages have skits and plays as well as vaudeville-type performances including magic, dancing, singing, and more.

As described above, the Faires are often made up of themed weekends for different, popular genres. You will see the Pirates, Fairies and Princesses, King Henry VIII, Magic & Wizards, Highland Scottish, Roman, Halloween, Celtic, Renaissance Christmas, May Festivals, Oktoberfest or Beer/Wine Festivals, and Knightly Tournaments, sometimes on the same day. With different themes every weekend, visitors can come again and again, getting subtly different entertainment. Many serious Rennies get season tickets and come multiple times during a festival even camping on site for after hours parties. The themes appeal to different visitors, drawing in larger audiences. For instance, Halloween and Fairy-themed weekends are popular destinations for parents to take their children. Little girls in fairy wings, with painted faces and flower wreaths woven into their hair (all available for purchase at the Faire) are very common, as are men in all their Scottish regalia and Harry Potter fans decked out in Hogwarts robes or dressed as their favorite characters. Children of all ages dress as pirates, from plastic swords to risqué pirate wench garb. Wine tasting festivals and Celtic arts draw in customers interested in soaking up culture and making a few purchases. All in all, the Faires attempt to cater to many tastes in a festive and playful way.

The food is important, and many Rennies talk about needing a fix of turkey drumsticks, the most ubiquitous of Faire food. Yes, as stitch counters and authenticity Nazis of all reenacting periods immediately point out, turkeys were not yet commonly available, raised, or eaten in Tudor England. Turkey drumsticks, beer, Pepsi, funnel cakes, and a variety of other foods served on sticks or dumped, gleaming, out of a deep fryer an onto a paper tray are not period. They are, however, festival food in America. As a result, they are Faire food. Faires are commercial vending and festivals first and foremost, and historical accuracy does not get in the way of a good time for all. The mixture of numerous genres and time periods is also distinctly festival in nature. Alcohol—especially theme-based beers, ales, meads, and wines—have their own fans, and are important draws for the Faires.

Jousting is one of the main attractions at most larger Faires. Indeed, armored knights and horses are prominent on advertisements for the Faires to play up this one-of-a-kind entertainment. A tourney field is maintained, with stands for the audience to view actual tournament-style jousting with lances, blunted swords or maces, armored knights, and large horses. Jousting is actually a competitive sport for many of the fighters, who make the rounds of numerous Faires much as rodeo riders compete on a circuit.

Characters and Types of Rennies

Rennies are the denizens of Renaissance Faires. Rennies themselves are the most tolerant of the reenacting paracultures. They actually engage Mundanes and enjoy "performing" their impressions for an audience. Whether they are customers (paying attendees of the Faires), workers hired by the

Faire, or merchants; Rennies seem blasé about historical inaccuracies and people who aren't joining in the reenacting. Unlike most reenacting paracultures, where the reenactors need others to join into the cooperative play to get the full experience, Rennies do not seem to have their sacred time disrupted by non-players. Unlike SCAdians and many war reenactors, for example, Rennies do not have trouble maintaining their impressions for an audience. In fact, many reported that they seem to need the performance and public experience to fully enjoy the festival. Many winked and told me that part of the fun was the exhibitionism—the experience of often-shy "nerds" (their term) being the flamboyant center of attention. The costumes, impressions, and routines Rennies perform are often fairly riske', adding an adult dimension to the entertainment and making the performances more exhilarating for reenactors who are often shy in their mundane lives.

Several groups populate the Faires. Faires have a staff who run and coordinate the Faires from year to year. This office staff works much of the year, maintaining the site and planning. They plan the themed weekends, hire and manage staff, coordinate entertainment, and bring in vendors. They are important to setting the tone and atmosphere of the Faire. Most Faire employees are temporaries hired to act as workers in food booths, to roam around the site per-forming and interacting with visitors, and performing on the many stages. Many are given particular characters and skits to learn. They are taught B.F.A. and instructed on how to enhance the Faire atmosphere for visitors. The staff usually contains at least one person to coordinate events such as field trips from local schools and weddings. Renaissance Faire weddings are very popular, and many Faires' wedding schedules are booked months if not a year in advance. The staff of the Faires assist by providing standard packages and inexpensive costume rentals for guests. Couples can choose festival food from the festive (turkey legs, beer, and pretzels) to the historically gourmet (reproduction Elizabethan or Tudor meals with fine wines or mead). There are many websites, books, and businesses oriented to provide Renaissance weddings.

Merchants and vendors are the backbone of the Faires. Their booths and merchandise provide interest, decoration, and draw in customers. Shopping and browsing are two of the major activi-ties at the Faires, and thus merchants are entertainment, decoration, and interactive displays all in one. Arts and crafts, books, clothing, toys, and esoteric materials are the most prevalent items sold. The arts and crafts include a huge variety of period-related artifacts such as ceramics, jewelry, candles, decorative objects, weaving, sculpture, henna painting, hair braiding (especially with little floral wreaths), and metal working. The genre may be historical European, fantasy-genre, Celtic, Scottish, or other. Books of all the themes from the Faires are available. In particular, visitors enjoy finding rare reproductions of their favorite time period or genre. Clothing from the simple and polyester to finely crafted historically-accurate is available in all Faire-related styles. Many visitors buy clothing or accessories and put them on while they are at the Faire to join in the fun. Toys for young and old are popular, from cute house elves to puzzles, toy swords, or pet dragons. Esoteric materials include herbal remedies; magical potions and paraphernalia; crystals; spell books; scented candles, lotions, and soaps; incense; psychics; ghost bottles; and more.

Merchants and many of the hired performers are interesting in that their reenacting world is more complex than the paying visitors. Paying visitors, as discussed above, do go to one or more faires, planning impressions and enjoying the culture. Merchants have actually made the Faires part of their livelihood. Many do it because they are craftsmen or have a passion for some of the types of merchandise at the Faires. Being merchants lets them make a living doing what they love. In order to do it full time, however, they have to become gypsies, travelling from Faire to Faire, across the country. They develop a unique traveling culture as their social group reunites at different Faires or as they return annually to a particular Faire. They have their own world behind the shop fronts, in their camper parks and in the back alleys that visitors do not see. At night, when the cannon sounds the end of the Faire, and the visitors leave, the Rennies have their own after party. Some merchants only come out for one or two Faires, using their vacation time for this one big event where they get to be their alternate personae. Most of all, the workers and merchants enjoy being with their own kind and feeling the sense of community. In a way, they have their private reenacting time much as the SCA and Civil War reenactors do, it's just not necessary that they be in character or perform then. The performances are for the public, the camaraderie is what afterhours socialization is about.

Unique Qualities of Faires their Reenactors

Renaissance Faires and the reenactors who inhabit them are quite different from Civil War and SCA reenactors. Despite this, there are some obvious similarities. Renaissance Faires do provide an environment for acting out a desired time-period fantasy. The fantasy part of the experience is both more open and more transparent, however. It is obviously fantasy given that supernatural creatures like witches, dragons, faeries, and theatrics are emphasized as the main themes of the Faires. That said, it is heavily populated with actors, consumerism, and entertainment in a way that differs from other types of reenactment genres. They are part reenatment, part festival, and all escapist entertainment. Other types of reenacting, such as that done in the SCA and Civil War genres, is also a fantasy, but it is heavily shrouded in attention to detail and reality. The very emphasis on achieving reality in personae, garb, and behavior by these types of reenactors is an attempt to pretend the fantasy is real. For, in their method acting, these reenactors want to achieve that period rush and escape into their shared reenacting fantasy. Rennies are already working within a festival environment, where roles are already reversed and rules are already suspended. They do not have to push the reality of the experience to achieve sacred time, for they can purchase it when they enter the gate.

Name _____ Date _____

I. Learning More About the Renaissance Faires

Assignment A: Basic Information

1. What are Renaissance Faires, and how long have they been around?

   _____

   _____

2. Where were the first U.S. Faire located and when?

   _____

   _____

3. How are Faires like old festivals from Europe?

   _____

   _____

   _____

4. What is **sacred time**?

   _____

   _____

5. What is the **liminal state** and when/how can you achieve it?

   _____

   _____

6. What is **role reversal** and how is it a part of festivals?

   _____

   _____

7. What time period and geographic/cultural area do Faires reenact?

   _____

8. What is B.F.A.? _____

9. What sorts of impressions or personae do Rennies adopt? _____

   _____

   _____

10. ... and how do these differ from SCA persona? _____

    _____

    _____

11. Ren Faires contain a lot of different types of reenactors—merchants, paying customers, competitors, and paid workers. How do these different groups fit into the reenactor mold?

    _____

    _____

    _____

    _____

12. How do Faires create an atmosphere for sacred time and role reversal, and how is this an important part of how Rennies achieve the period rush?

    _____

    _____

    _____

    _____

    _____

Assignment B: Researching the Faires Online

There are several online sources for information on Faires. Renaissance.com is a good source, and you can simply type "Faire" or "Renaissance Faire" into your search engine. Several particular Faires are described in the chapter and have their own websites. There are even blogs where hardcore Rennies can hash about the different Faires.

Find a Faire near you or of particular interest to you.

1. What is its name? _____

   and website? _____

2. When and where is the Faire scheduled? _____

3. Look at the websites and advertisements for Renaissance Faires. What images are used? What key words are used to entice audiences?

   _____

   _____

4. What are the stated goals of the Faires?

   _____

   _____

5. What sorts of activities or attractions are available to Ren Faire attendees?

   _____

   _____

6. What behaviors and practices are emphasized?

   _____

7. How do the Ren Faires compare to the SCA events described from the previous chapter? (Make sure to state how they are 1) similar to, and 2) different from, SCA events.)

   _____

   _____

8. What genres or characters are represented at the Faire?

_____

_____

9. How do these characters and genres differ from SCA events?

_____

_____

_____

10. How do Rennies attempt to achieve the period rush? (Hint: where and in what setting do they like to become their persona?)

_____

_____

_____

11. Are Rennies more privately-oriented or publically-oriented in their activities? What role does observation by a public play in the experience for Rennies?

_____

_____

_____

_____

_____

12. How are Ren Faire personae different from other reenactors' impressions?

_____

_____

_____

_____

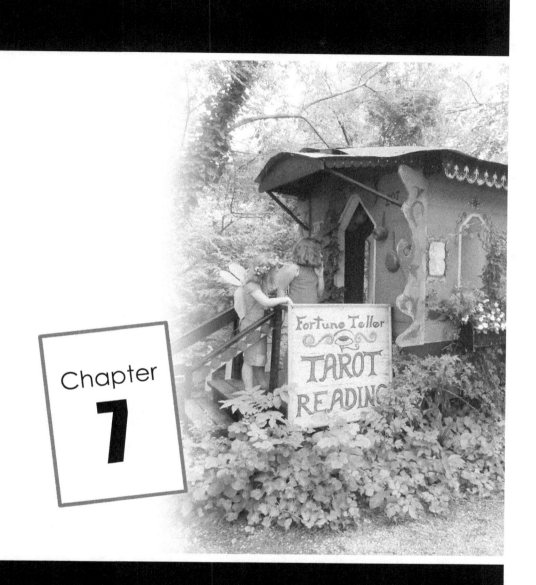

Chapter

7

Civil War Reenactors

Introduction: Civil War Reenacting: It's not What You Think

When historical reenactors are mentioned, American Civil War reenactors are one of the most likely types that come to mind for most Americans. I've been collecting freelists of types of reenactors from students for over a decade, and most students have heard of Civil War reenactors—even if they only know two types. Civil War reenactors are widely known, but they are also poorly understood. These same people who list CW reenactors are also likely to state that they have a negative initial reaction, even though they often revise that to a positive reaction after reading about them. While this is partly due to their popularity—Civil War reenactors are still the single most common genre, numbering around 40,000–60,000 active reenactors—it is also due to their unfortunate portrayal in popular culture and the media. As discussed in Chapter 1, CW reenactors are often incorrectly portrayed as racists and white supremacists who want to glorify slavery and treasonous rebellion—as well as recreate a society with white supremacy and racial discrimination. While some white supremacists do appropriate symbols from the Civil War and the Confederacy, this is not an accurate portrayal of most CW reenactors.

In addition to negative portrayals as racists, reenactors are also commonly used as a comedic device in the media. When a writer wants to portray a fictional character as goofy, silly, or mentally unhinged, one of the common tricks is just to make him a Civil War reenactor. Much fun is had at the expense of the reenactor, mocking their love of historical artifacts, having the straight character play act in the funny Civil War costumes; and, of course, making fun of the reenactors going out and playing at war. It's a standard comedic device, and while even the writers often say it's only in fun, this consistently mocking portrayal deeply affects how reenactors are perceived by outsiders. The media almost always portrays reenactors as men, despite the fact that many females are involved in all types of reenacting. The sad thing is that this character is accepted as a buffoon- out of touch, socially deficient, and often just plain nuts.

Scholarly literature is not much better; Academia has paid little attention to reenacting phenomena. As discussed in Chapter 1, what little is out there is often unflattering and shallow. Academic historians often react very negatively to reenactors, even though they are closely associated with living history and active fundraising for historic site preservation. A few scholars have studied reenactors, however. Jenny Thompson's *War Games: Inside the World of Twentieth Century War Reenactors* (2004) stands out as a thorough, in-depth study of 20th century reenactors, though it only touches on Civil War reenacting. Thompson's study is the exception. It is unbiased, showing how an ethical and professional ethnography should be presented. The most popular supposedly ethnographic work on Civil War reenactors and other affiliated groups has a fatal flaw. Tony Horwitz's *Confederates in the Attic: Dispatches from the Unfinished Civil War* is not an ethnography and does not follow any of the ethical guidelines of anthropological ethnographic fieldwork. This is a book written by a journalist in the New Journalism style. Ethical anthropological research does not ridicule or belittle the culture being studied. Horwitz did do interviews and participant observation with reenactors, going with them on reenactments and gaining their trust. He abused that trust in a way not acceptable in anthropological research by using the insight and information he gained to make fun of the hardcore reenactors he befriended. Horwitz's key informants were hardcore reenactors, and he emphasizes the more extreme version of reenacting. He compounds the ethical crime of mocking his informants by mixing in other Southern identity movements and issues. In between segments on reenactors, he blends in interviews from non-reenacting white supremacists and people involved in a murder related to displaying the Confederate Battle Flag, intentionally equating reenactors with white supremacists. Racism is not accepted in the reenactor community. Reenactors and the teenagers with Confederate flags on their pick-ups are not the same thing, and reenactors are not part of the as the Southern identity movement or supremacist groups. (If you *do* want to read more ethnographic work on Southern identity and white supremacist groups, my colleague Dianne Dentice has several articles on the topic. We've even collaborated on some projects exploring the differences.) Horwitz does a disservice to all of his sources by intimating that the groups are synonymous. His book serves to strengthen the negative and uninformed stereotypes many people have of reenactors.

If they are not the simplistic gun nuts or racists portrayed in the media, what then, are Civil War reenactors? They are many things. Civil War reenactors are a diverse group of men and women who come together to bring the people and events of the U.S. Civil War to life again, if only for a brief glimpse into life in the past. They do it for many reasons, most simply to understand and experience a bit of what the past was like. As a culture, many Americans are fascinated with the Civil War as well as particularly the antebellum period. It stands as one of the fairy tale genres for Americans—our long ago mythical times. Europe has castles, knights, and princesses. Americans have cowboys, Davy Crockett, and the mythology of the Civil War: generals, soldiers, Scarlet O'Hara, Rhett Butler, and drawling Southern ladies in hoop skirts.

My purpose in this chapter is to do away with any preconceived notions you may have about this particular group being a bunch of redneck hillbillies or raving white supremacists stomping around in the woods with black powder rifles. As with each group we discuss, these are real people, with faults, flaws and fine points of their own. They are also enthusiastic, honorable, smart, well-read men and women from many cultural backgrounds who are committed to historical and cultural preservation. They love history, culture, and passing on traditions. As such, they have been incredibly helpful with my research and open to being ethnographic subjects and partners. As an anthropologist, it is rare to study a group so willing to share their culture and allow an outsider access. It is my hope that you will gain respect for these people and their love of historical heritage, just as I did.

Fieldwork with Civil War Reenactors

When I was beginning my dissertation fieldwork as a graduate student at University of Missouri looking for traditional herbal practitioners, I initially observed and researched multiple types of reenactors, including the Civil War folks. I was surprised to note the regional differences between Missouri reenactment groups and those with which I had been familiar from central and Southern Arkansas. I observed Civil War reenactors in and around central Missouri and found that they were different in several ways. The first big surprise was all of the blue coats! In central and northern Missouri, the Union soldiers were the good guys, and monuments stretched from Kansas City to St. Louis memorializing Union generals such as

Reenactors rest against a fence at Gettysburg. Photographs are often staged to capture the 'feeling' of actual Civil War photography.
Copyright Jupiter Images.

Sheridan, Sherman, and Grant—men who appeared as villains in such classics of southernism as Margaret Mitchell's 1936 classic *"Gone with the Wind"* and regional southern folklore. Yankees were the heroes to the east, north and west of me, yet in south-central Missouri, there were die-hard Confederate reenactors and even Missouri-German-immigrant militia reenactors.

Even more interesting, I noticed that the same men often unloading both Union and Confederate regalia—portraying either side as needed for the reenactment. And . . . that the reenactors were jovial and friendly with each other, even when they made Union vs. Confederate jokes. These men (and women . . . I had not realized the importance of women in Civil War reenacting before my fieldwork) enjoyed each other's company and were very peacefully and amicably reenacting the war known for its bitter divisiveness. The war in which brother fought brother is now reenacted by men who trade coats and impressions partway through the day in the interest of historical accuracy. The same old Civil War reenacting I had taken for granted during my childhood was much more complex than I had realized before I began observing them from an anthropological perspective. These historical reenactors had a culture not readily apparent to outsiders. I found that I, myself, had many pre-conceived ideas about Civil War reenactors that were naïve and simplistic. It took many hours of fieldwork, observation, and research to gain a more holistic understanding of Civil War reenactors.

My own enculturation had shaped my perceptions of Civil War folklore and symbols. My brother and sister are both history buffs, and we come from a family where regional history and family folklore are important topics. Both of my grandmothers were very interested in both family history and southern history surrounding the Civil War and reconstruction. My mother's family has unusually long generation spans, (my siblings and I are only the 8th generation since 1732 and my maternal grandmother's grandfather fought and was killed in the Civil War.) Talking to my maternal grandmother Rose about her family's involvement in the war and the hard years that followed made the era seem much more immediate and personal. Rose Beatrice Ashcraft Hanson Bunyard knew survivors of the war firsthand and could pass on the stories from her grandparents. The war was real to us as it is to many southerners because of these deep familial connections to real family members and the land beneath our feet. In areas where the war was fought—North and South–, Americans grow up being able to stand on the actual landscape of the war, the stories of their ancestors' involvement made real. My brother is particularly interested in both history and genealogy, and spent many long hours working on genealogy with both grandmothers. Coupled with his career as an officer in the U.S. Army, he is particularly well-read and knowledgeable about military history. My sister is both a history buff and a devourer of all things Southern—from history to literature to custom. Though all of these sources, I was raised and enculturated with a good deal of lore from the Civil War as a part of my social and cultural identity.

With this family background, I found myself talking about my research, and especially the reenactors, with my family. I think that my work fueled the interest already sparked by the reenactors my brother had observed giving living history demonstrations at the museums and libraries around his hometown. My brother started by asking questions, and then, as he got to know the Civil War reenactors, became interested in reenacting himself. His inquiries were met with cheerful helpfulness and warm invitations to participate. One of the first things he told me after talking with several was "These guys are pretty cool—very nice, and they really know their history!" He was hooked, and found himself a new hobby and a group of friends in the process. . . . my brother was beginning his own transformation into a Civil War reenactor. We talked a lot, because we actually had someone family to talk to reenacting about, and our different experiences struck both of us as interesting. We ended up comparing notes, and he kept saying that I really needed to write about reenactors—they really were so different than people imagined.

We probably had our first really enlightening conversations about ethnographic method and anthropological fieldwork during this time. My brother immediately made the same connection I'd written in my own field notes. Reenactors are about participant observation and cooperative play. To take the analysis further, they are groups of participant observers who all agree to play together under a set of agreed-upon rules. As our parallel experiences progressed—my fieldwork, and his becoming a reenactor, I wrote in my notes that reenactors, except perhaps many of my Renaissance Faire consultants (more about that in the chapter on Ren Faire reenactors!) were really attempting to participant observe or "method act" their way into the emic perspective. Reenactors enculturate, or become part of their paraculture, in much the same way that anthropologists do ethnographic fieldwork. They join in, they participate and become part of the society by doing. In the process, they begin to understand and belong. The anthropologist doing ethnographic work differs from a person truly joining a new society in that he or she must also hold onto the etic perspective during this process, retaining a part of self that is the "professional stranger" (Agar 1996, Bernard 2006).

As we learned more about reenacting, we both encountered various versions of two phenomena: *the period rush* and *escaping the everyday* as goals of the reenactment process. Escaping the everyday through reenacting is a common goal for reenactors. Again and again, reenactors describe

Union Civil War Reenactors relax and chat next to a warm campfire. Soldier standing in right corner is Tom Ezell, who contributed greatly to the research as a key consultant. He did point out the smiles in this photo and explain "Yankees have better coffee!" Civil War reenactors use authentic rations (food) whenever possible, from awful coffee to stale hardtack.
Photo by Steve Shore.

reenacting as a form of therapeutic escapism that helps them to relieve stress. As with the SCA, many Civil War reenactors describe their chosen historical period as being more gracious, with people held to codes of honor and politeness. Male reenactors, in particular, like "treating ladies like ladies" and "being allowed to act the gentleman." Female reenactors report that, indeed, they find gentlemanly behavior amongst the male reenactors to be very appealing and feel very appreciated by this treatment.

What is "the period rush" for Civil War reenactors, though? It is much the same as the period rush and sacred time experiences described by SCA and Ren Faire reenactors. For Civil War reenactors, they describe it as "being there, in the moment." They describe actually feeling the reality of the moment/time being reenacted. Much like SCA reenactors, they are able to lose their conscious awareness of themselves as their modern selves and feel like they are someone living through that event. They feel like they have captured the feeling, the emotion, and the experience of being part of the time. In so doing, they get a rush of exhilaration and bonding with their fellow reenactors as well as the actual people who originally experienced the events of the war. CW reenactors describe the same feelings of communitas and sacred time that the other reenactors describe. The rituals of re-creating their characters and co-modifying the experiences of people who lived through the Civil War create that out of time, shared experience that all reenactors seek. For historical reenactors, it is a form of experiential time travel.

The War on Replay: History of Civil War Reenacting

Memorializing the war was common in the Union states following the war. Parades, memorial parks, statues, and holidays memorializing the war were common in both the North and South. Former Union soldiers formed the Grand Army of the Republic (GAR), with their descendants forming societies such as the Sons of Union Veterans of the Civil War (SUVCW) and the Auxiliary to the SUVCW as the years passed. The Grand Army of the Republic was particularly known for helping with charity, hospitals, and orphanages. Other Northern groups included the Loyal Legion, The Soldiers and Sailors National Union League, and other regimental or regional societies of veterans. The United Confederate Veterans formed in the South, with the United Daughters of the Confederacy, Children of the Confederacy, and the Sons of Confederate Veterans and numerous other smaller patriotic groups following over the years. Veterans from both sides of the war often participated in anniversary parades and public ceremonies. Though they also were social organizations, these groups did and continue to have a great interest in preserving and memorializing events and materials from the Civil War. A drive through many of the larger Civil War battlefield parks reveals multiple and impressive memorials, many of them donated by these groups. Countless other small historical markers and plaques commemorating Civil War events—especially battles and cemeteries—are scattered throughout the eastern and southern United States.

Veterans and these ancestor-based groups commemorated major (and even minor) battles with parades, speeches, and community events over the years. As the years passed, the war and its events were reinterpreted to suit current sociopolitical needs—particularly the heroic sacrifices necessary to forge a strong, unified, and "modern" or progressive country. The first reenactments seem to have been "Sham battles" that were even put on by the military as a way for new soldiers to gain a better understanding of the great battles and experiences of the Civil War Hadden 1999). The first large-scale reenactments occurred from 1911–1915, as fiftieth anniversaries of the Civil War were observed throughout the country with the admonition that forgetting them could result in a weaker, less patriotic country (*Harper's Weekly,* April 22, 1911, 4 as cited in Franklin 1962).

The fiftieth anniversaries and reenactments were observed by holding reunions at major battlefields like Bull Run, Antietam, Gettysburg, and Vicksburg. Indeed, these battlefields host some of the largest and most noticed (by the public) reenactments and memorial services today. The end of the semicentennial festivities and commemorations was somewhat sober, however, as World War I loomed. World War II cast a shadow over the 75th anniversaries of the Civil War, and as all but the very last few veterans had died by this time, little public ceremony or public attention marked these anniversaries.

The centennial anniversaries of the Civil War in the 1960s, however, did not compete with a world war and were lavishly celebrated. A historian writing at the time (John Hope Franklin), noted that *"One searches in vain for an event in our history that has been commemorated with the same intense and elaborate preparation that characterizes the Civil War centennial* (Franklin 1962, 103)" Among the preparations were national, state, and local Civil War Centennial Commissions, complete with budgets in the millions of dollars. Battlefields were set aside as parks, historical markers were erected, particularly in the former Confederacy. *"Impressive buildings-have been constructed to house the mementoes of the Confederate effort and to tell the story of the Lost Cause. Sham battles are being staged to stimulate the imagination and to encourage viewers to second-guess the outcome.*" (Franklin 1962, pg 104). Even during the centennial events, American responses to the commemorations were divided. While many threw themselves into the anniversary events with zeal and enthusiasm, others criticized the celebrations as juvenile and vulgar—a bizarre and inappropriate way to commemorate a national nightmare. Descendants of Americans from both sides of the war agreed, however: the horrors of the divisive Civil War were a national tragedy, but the war was the defining event, the shared nightmare, that forged a shared national identity for the United States. Confederate flags and paraphernalia were everywhere, but the people wielding them were *Americans,* intensely patriotic to the United States even while they glorified the dream of the Confederacy and the romance of the antebellum South.

After the dust settled on the Civil War Centennial events, we were left with a rich network of battlefield parks, museums, and memorials. Most of all, we were left with romantic, celebratory national memories of the war as the archetype of American heroism and historical legacy. Actual reenacting of the type that gave rise to today's reenacting traditions seems to have gotten started around the time of the early 1960s with the centennial anniversary of the war. Most of today's historical reenactors have little in common with the gaudy and often wildly inaccurate reenactments staged during the Civil War for public consumption. And, much like the "Cowboys and Indians" portrayed in pop culture and by Hollywood which have little to do with accurate portrayals of Native American Indians; Civil War-themed movies, novels, and television shows had little basis in historical accuracy. Historic reenactors often groan in dismay at these "Gone With the Wind" knockoffs and the Farbs they attract. How then, did the serious modern reenactors evolve if they did not come from this tradition?

Reenactors cross arms at Gettyburg, PA during a public reenactment. Gettysburg has some of the largest Civil War reenactments.
Copyright Jupiter Images.

Civil War reenactors who are intensely interested in historical accuracy and preservation are more a product of the living history movement that began with museums, state and national parks interpretation, and public education in the 1980s. **Living history** is an educational tool in which people create a historically accurate impression (character) and then not only demonstrate correct historical recreations, but interact with spectators and "interpret" or explain the differences between the time period being presented and modern understanding. Many of the first scholar reenactors began as museum tour guides, teachers, or historians who were attempting to 'liven up' history to make it more accessible for public education. According to Jay Anderson in *Time Machines: The World of Living History* (1984) and an earlier article in *American Quarterly* (1982), living history practitioners can be categorized into three groups. Anderson categorizes living history into 1) museum professionals seeking a new way of educating, 2) experimental archaeologists conducting research into past practices, and 3) "history buffs" who reenact recreationally.

Museums began using living exhibits, or guides dressed up in historical garments, performing tasks or displaying skills from different time periods, as early as the 1890s in Europe. Colonial Williamsburg established live interpretation with historical reenactment in the U.S. when it opened in the 1920s and 30s. The popularity and success of Colonial Williamsburg established period reenactment and live interpretation as a gold standard for quality public history. "Living history" as a method of public education was adopted by the National Park Service in the 1960s and 1970s, as well as at several other historical or cultural institutions. These living history exhibits were quite different than stunt costumes or Hollywood-style entertainment. While the costumes and activities were designed to excite the public and capture their imagination, the goal was education. As a result, great care was taken to provide historically accurate presentations. Accurate reproduction sets, artifacts, clothing, even speech and behaviors were the goal. Living history reenactors attempted to "get into character" much as a method actor, by immersing themselves in detail. Living historians researched history, folklore, and technology to gain a more holistic understanding of their 'characters.' "Interpretation" was an important element at museums and historic sites as well. Park and museum interpreters were attempting to translate the perspective of people from a particular time period and context so that visitors could gain insight into what life would have been like in the past. The idea was that this would not only provide a richer, more fulfilling experience for the visitor, but would also help the public to form an emotional and personal link.

Historical reenactment can also be a research tool. Some questions about the abilities of past peoples and their technology can be tested by recreating them. Replica ships of various sorts have been constructed and sailed to test their seaworthiness and range. Replica weapons and tools can be used to test their effectiveness as well as what types of tool marks they would leave. In this way, archaeologists have been able to interpret tool marks on artifacts, bones, and buildings. Past agricultural, artistic, architectural, food preparation, and medical techniques have been tested in this way. When several techniques are proposed, reenacting the different techniques under controlled simulations allows scholars to test which leaves evidence that most closely matches archeological evidence. The newly revealed methods are then often shared with living history exhibits for public education.

Finally, Anderson categorizes the third type of living history practitioner as those who do it as 'play.' He includes the North-South Skirmish Association, a group that began reenacting Civil War battles in the 1950s among a list that includes other early reenactment groups like the American Mountain Men and the Society for Creative Anachronism in the 1960s and the Brigade of the American Revolution in the 1970s. Anderson does credit the popularity of living history participation as a recreational activity for escapism, but he emphasizes that it is healthy and beneficial recreation. It is play, but it is not juvenile. Instead, it is an opportunity for people to spend their leisure time in a social environment that better suits their preferences and personality.

Modern Civil War Reenactors

Serious, or hardcore reenactors that attend several events a year, owe much of their culture to living history reenactors. Though there are many reenactors whose activities are purely recreational without a great deal of scholarly investment, these tend to be the reenactors who attend the occasional public event recreating a large battle. Hardcore reenactors invest a great deal of their time in research, public education, and interaction among other reenactors.

Today's reenactors frequently overlap into more than one of Anderson's categories. His recreational living history practitioners are much more cavalier about historical accuracy than the bulk of today's reenactors. In the parlance of serious Civil War reenactors, they sound like FARBS. The term 'Farbs' has a few different translations, some kinder than others. "Far be it from authentic" is the most common, though many gentlemanly reenactors will offer up a polite "Far be it from me to question his attempts." "Fast and Researchless Buying" and a few much ruder translations exist as well, though most of the gentlemen I interviewed were far too gentlemanly to repeat such things in front of a lady or to treat their fellows with disrespect. On a different note, Farb is sometimes reputed to derive from a German slang term referring to a carnival-goer or clown. Unless one of the first users of the term is found, we may never know the exact origins. The meaning, however, is clear among serious reenactors. That said, what is a Farb? To be accused of being a Farb means that your gear, clothing, behaviors, etc . . . are NOT PERIOD. I type this in all caps to emphasize the seriousness of this charge. To not be historically-accurate to the time period being reenacted violates the whole point of historical reenacting. If you are 'not period' you are not doing your part in joining the others in the right frame. You clash; you might jar others from the shared reality of the reenactment. Great effort is expended to enjoy the ambiance of shared play. A Farb who shows up with sneakers, blue jeans, a polyester jacket, or an Ipod can ruin the mood for everyone. And maintaining that mood, that shared reality, is the way that reenactors find that period rush together. Not all reenactors are hostile to Farbs and are genuinely accepting to anyone who wants to honestly join in, regardless of their ability to invest in a complete set of gear. Farbs probably do most closely resemble the earliest of Civil War reenactors in many ways as old veterans and their sons, daughters, and grandchildren dressed in their old gear or in home-made copies of uniforms and dresses to participate in anniversary commemorations of the war. Costume balls in the South held by the Sons of Confederate Veterans or the United Daughters of the Confederacy were much more Farb than most of today's serious historical reenactments.

So the question is, are Farbs bad? To the serious Stitch Counter (see below), Farbs are treated with great disdain and efforts are made to reform, control, or exclude them from events they might "ruin" for the serious. Most reenactors are fairly gentlemanly about them, agreeing that they have their place and the right to reenact as they choose. So-called Farbs are often descendants of war veterans and may be members of local historical groups. They often carry influence and can be quite beneficial to the cause of preservation. Though they like "showy spectacles" for the public to observe and do like to get dressed up in very showy period costumes, they are also generous and interested purveyors of local cultural preservation. They are more likely to be behind events such as balls, parades, and publicly-viewed "staged" reenactments. These events do reach the public, recruit new reenactors, and most of all—raise money to preserve historic sites. Farbs have a very important part in reenactor society, even if they are quite different in other ways from the other reenactors.

On the opposite end of the spectrum of Civil War reenactors are Stitch Counters. **Stitch Counters** are found in all types of historical reenacting, though they are frequently called 'Authenticity Nazis' in the S.C.A. A Stitch Counter does exactly what the name implies and more. He or she wants to see the inner seams and hems of garments to inspect the stitches. Were the stitches made in the appropriate style to the time period? What type of thread was used? What about the weave of the fabric? Cut of the pattern? The dyes used? Stitch Counters demand period perfection. They purchase or create patterns from actual historical garments. They closely inspect historical documents. I have met many who spin wool, weave fabric, and dye fabric in a historically-accurate manner. Buttons and belt buckles made from original molds (or duplicates made through reverse molds created from an authentic artifact) are a hot item on eBay and other reenacting mercantiles. If they can't manufacture materials from scratch, they will often get as close as possible and treat those materials to achieve an end product as close as possible to an accurate-appearing reproduction. Stitch Counters are chasing the fine details or authenticity through their artifacts, and this quest helps them to get "that period feel." They are the 'hardcore' reenactors that are beyond the casual description of 'history buffs.' The degree of detail they pursue and the sheer amount of knowledge they acquire in their quest begs the question: are they amateurs? Professional historians can definitely say they are amateurs by definition because they usually do not have formal degrees in history. Anthropologically, however, there are different categories that can be applied. Expert and Novice, or non-expert, are categories used for cultural knowledge domains. In the domain of their historical period, many reenactors are definitely experts, regardless of whether they have formal degrees in history or costume design. They have a great deal of specialized knowledge and are acknowledged as experts by their peers.

Most reenactors fall somewhere in the middle of the spectrum between Farbs and Stitch Counters. Sometimes called **Mainstreamers**, they do strive for historical accuracy and invest a great deal of time into their gear, but no one fears they will crack up if they discover a piece of synthetic material amongst someone's gear. 'History buffs' though they may be, most of these mainstream reenactors also have a great deal of expertise and are very involved in scholarly study of Civil War history, costumes, customs, and artifacts. That, in fact, leads us to the next topic: Just what do Civil War reenactors do?

What Do Civil War Reenactors Do?

In general, most Civil War reenactors spend a great deal of time doing research. They read histories, diaries, books, and newspapers from the Civil War era and the surrounding years. They read histories written about the Civil War after the fact. They study clothing patterns, technical diagrams or machinery, tools, and technology. They try to learn what people ate and how, their customs, their practices, their perspectives. In short, they try to learn as much ethnographic information as possible about the time period. They often write up reports to share with other reenactors through their newsletters or at meetings. Best of all, this research and hard homework is considered fun! Reenactors' research is a part of a social learning atmosphere. Sharing and seeking knowledge gives them a medium for interaction, cooperation, and reciprocity. Social status among other reenactors can be gained through scholarly prowess and/or skills at period technology.

Outside of formal social events or meetings, reenactors talk on the phone, hang out and chat, and interact via the internet. Research and the accompanying discussions in which reenactors share what they know and discuss their knowledge makes up the heart of the social component of reenacting. Being part of a reenacting community involves a great deal of socialization. This is probably the first misconception to dispel. Common negative comments about reenactors include "Get a life", "get out more", and "grow up." Reenactors do "have a life" and do "get out more". They have busy social schedules that are much more "grown up" than their detractors guess.

This social activity ranges from solitary research activities to group interactive activities. Individuals share what they have learned with others in the group (and often on the internet through newsletters and websites) through reports, summaries, talks, and demonstrations. New recruits are mentored by more experienced reenactors to help them learn reenactor customs as well as the technical knowledge to do living history. Group meetings often include historical lectures, the sharing of new information, and discussions of how to help with local, regional, and national historic preservation. Reenactors are often members of several organizations dedicated to history, battlefield preservation, and education. They will volunteer to put on living history demonstrations at local libraries, schools, cemeteries, monuments, festivals, museums, and parks. They will often work as extras for local tourism films and photos. They will reach directly into their pockets to make donations to preserve and maintain historic sites. The battle reenactments that catch the public eye are usually held to raise money and awareness for maintenance and preservation of parks and memorials. They physically clean up trash and debris in old cemeteries and hold public memorials. When they are offered a fee for reenacting (as in the case of movies or television shows), the groups will often agree upon a suitable project to which they donate the proceeds. In short, reenactors tend to be very civic minded, contributing time, effort, and money to protecting cultural heritage without compensation.

In living history demonstrations, reenactors dress and act as a person from the Civil War would have, yet interact with the public. They answer questions, show their gear, and show how things worked. Spectators to the museum, school, park or other event often want to see and touch their clothing or gear up close. Often, they have food or drink samples or works in progress to show manufacturing skills. They talk, telling stories and trying to bring the past to life in a way that static displays do not. Often, Civil War reenactors are invited by museums and schools, working in cooperation with them to improve public turnout and satisfaction. Seeing "real" people and things from the Civil War brings it to life for people, especially children.

One thing that frequently surprises people is that many African Americans are involved in Civil War reenacting. This shouldn't be surprising, given the importance of the war to African American history as well as American history in general. The movie *Glory* brought African American contributions to the Union Army into the public mind, and real reenactors played many of the extras in that movie. African Americans also reenact as Confederate soldiers, for many African Americans were on both sides, both voluntarily and non-voluntarily. Though some soldiers were ex-slaves or escaped slaves, many were freeborn Northerners. Not all African Americans fighting on the Confederate side were conscripted slaves, though. Some were fighting for their homes willingly. The role of African Americans in the Civil War is a complex and fascinating topic, and that many men and women are exploring through reenacting. Racism in any form is seriously taboo in the reenacting community, and most groups prominently display prohibitions on any form of white supremacy or degradation of anyone based on their race. Tolerance and balancing both sides is often enhanced by having reenactors change sides and play Union one day, Confederate the next. Despite playing at a bitter civil war, reenactors are actually very friendly and agreeable with each other.

Reenactors also reenact events and practices from the Civil War. They cook, sew, manufacture, sing, and dance. Garments are very important for reenacting. While many purchase their clothing and gear, creating clothing is a very popular pastime among reenactors. Males and females will both work together to make costumes. My mother was quite tickled that my brother came to her for sewing lessons. He and his buddies acquired period patterns and all worked together to make their uniforms for an upcoming event. They started with period-correct cloth (no polyester, please). They searched out the correct types of fabric, some of it mail-ordered from merchants specializing in historically-accurate fabrics and dyes. They cut the patterns (a nerve-wracking business when that precious fabric is $70 a yard or more), pieced them, and sewed. They were very proud of their seams and the cut and fit of their coats. It

Reenactors study artifacts preserved from the Civil War for detail.
Copyright Jupiter Images.

took tremendous effort to get all of the details right, and the experience created a social bond among the men who worked together. Such sewing parties and similar meetings to work on artifacts and practice maneuvers are common social events.

Females also reenact the Civil War. Though some do battlefield reenactment, many of them reenact civilians and medical personnel. Women do sometimes reenact as soldiers. Most of them work hard to "pass as boys" as would have been necessary during the war. Female reenactors usually choose personae that are either local women or the wives and daughters of soldiers. They cook for the soldiers, nurse the wounded, bring water, and attend the all-important celebratory balls at battle reenactments. Though they are outnumbered by the males, female Civil War reenactors are a very important part of the society.

Civilian reenactors are common as well. Civilian roles include non-combatants such as local townspeople, government officials, merchants, and medical practitioners. The merchants are actually merchants selling specialized goods to reenactors. Part of the fun of a reenactment is shopping through an assortment of buttons, belt buckles, weapons, cutlery, fabrics, canteens, inkwells, lockets, tents, sabers. . . . You name it. The sheer variety of period merchandise at reenactments and through online merchants is staggering. Merchants sell gear and wardrobes in a range of authenticity from Flashy Farb to Stitch Counter perfection for the enthusiastic reenactor. They also sell food.

Period fare is an important part of the reenactment experience. Soldiers will attempt to eat historically-accurate meals and drinks when reenacting to truly capture that authentic feeling. A great deal of research goes into what was actually available at a given battle or time for both Union and Confederate troops. General consensus is that Yankees did eat better most of the time, with more reliable supply lines and the greater resources of the North, especially toward the end of the war. Good coffee and plentiful bacon are a matter of pride among Union reenactors, especially those who just took a turn at being Confederate. Great pride is taken in scrounging up foraged food and replicating the humble diet of the Confederate troops, however. Some reenactment coordinators use a sense of historical humor when provisioning the troops—such as providing the soldiers with chickens . . . live chickens that they must catch. The provision boxes often contain a historically-accurate assortment. Reenactor are left to use their ingenuity and equipment (period only, please) to Iron Chef some meals for their troops with their period provisions. If the fare is miserable, it adds to the experience, but it is often a matter of great pride to provide a delicious campfire feast from humble ingredients after a hard day of fighting. Reenactors bond over the campfire, sharing food and conversation.

The authenticity of the gear comes into play with environmental conditions. Soldiers sleep on the ground, with a blanket and perhaps a small tent. Whether it is cold, hot, mosquito-y, raining, sleeting, or lovely; they endure as the soldiers did. I am told, however that there is a limit. My brother told of one reenactment where they set up camp by the water's edge on a lovely site. Just as the park rangers left, they mentioned that the gator population had really been on the rise in recent years. As twilight fell, nervous reenactors watched for the gleam of alligator eyes and jumped at each splash or plop from the water. Daylight found most of them sleeping in the cabs or beds of their trucks. After all, wouldn't a real soldier have had the sense to take shelter from gators? Abandoned barns or churches on reenactment sites, park benches, old church pews, merchants' tables, and in one case a demonstrator's coffin have all served as shelter in howling thunderstorms. Despite their efforts, reenactors often endure miserable conditions and awaken to fight in the morning just as the real soldiers did. Enduring miserable weather, mud, and blistered feet from authentic footwear all add to the authenticity of the experience. The serious reenactor is on a quest to understand what it would have been like for the real person at that time. The physical reality actually helps to break out of the modern self and experience the subjective state of mind and body.

When a reenactor endures hardship, it is "hardcore," a mark of pride in enduring for authenticity. Hardcore reenacting may include marching barefoot, rough conditions, physical discomfort, and pushing endurance. I've observed reenactors huddled in pouring rain, working despite mud to their knees, wearing wool in 100+ degree blistering sun and more. The admiring and macho affirmation of reenactors going extreme is "Hardcore!"

The War on Replay

Finally, reenactors go out and recreate battles from the Civil War. They do their best, given the limitations of numbers and park regulations, to retrace the movements and events of battles. Gettysburg, Vicksburg, Antietam, Shiloh . . . and many many more battles are reenacted. Some are recreated annually, others every few years or even once a decade. Particular anniversaries are usually larger events, though this varies. The public can usually come out for one or two "battle displays" on a Saturday with a possible repeat showing on Sunday afternoon. They spread out, sometimes on bleachers, often on lawn chairs and blankets they have brought, and photograph the big battles. Civilian reenactors often have living history demonstrations nearby that cater to the public as well. Often there is a nearby museum or historical park with their displays. People can make donations that go to the maintenance of the memorials or museums. The whole event is a public festival. That's the reenactment the public sees.

The real event experience, however, goes on behind the scenes for the reenactors. They arrive Friday night from their jobs and set up camp. The campsites are usually off in the fields, away from the town or museum. Campsites are kept as authentic as possible, and the reenactors form up into their assigned groups, getting to know each other. They visit with each other, cook dinner, and generally socialize in a period environment. The reenactors' camps are liminal— separating them from their everyday lives and letting them enter that period environment so they can get into the period mood together. They form up and move around in the morning, often playing at a few skirmishes or other events—all out of sight of the modern audience. When they do reenact, they have often managed to become involved enough in the play that they are not jarred out of the period rush by the spectators. It allows them to stay in character and enjoy the event despite the outsiders.

This is not to say that they never ham it up for the public. They do enjoy putting on a good show, both for the spectators and for each other. The art of dying is important. Though it's important to "die" in a way that's visually impressive to the public, it's also important to die in a comfortable place. Contorted in the bright noonday sun may look great, but the guy's got to hold that pose. "The smart soldier finds a nice shady tree with a good view and dies comfortably settled." The boom of the blanks in their guns and cannons is always good for spectacle, and a good "rebel yell" is important to the thrill of combat. These aren't completely for show. The noise, the smoke, the rush of running through the woods or across the field in full battle engagement is a huge part of the rush. It's a way to get caught up in the excitement and fear, and it's the reason they actually reenact battles instead of just marching around town squares. In fact, several battle reenactments do not have a public component. They are purely for the reenactors. Even in these reenactments, great care is taken to use blanks or safe cartridges and practice strict gun safety. The guns are real, but the bullets are not and the safeties are on. Nobody wants to accidentally harm another reenactor. These are bloodless battles.

Of course, I'd be remiss if I forgot to mention the balls. Most battle reenactments have a ball on Saturday night. It gives a chance for males and females to interact, for relaxed partying, and different garments. Reenactors who enjoy it replicate the music, and most of them try to dance and socialize. The gentlemen get to be gentlemen for the ladies, and a sense of the graciousness of the antebellum period is recaptured for a night. Even the grumpier super-masculine guys confess to enjoying the balls occasionally, though they say they only do it "for the ladies."

Why This War?

Why do so many people choose to reenact this particular war? What is so attractive, so salient, about the American Civil War? When I ask reenactors, they say that it speaks to them—pulls at their imagination. It is salient to them in a way that is both immediate and distantly romantic. The Civil War or "War Between the States" is immediate to many Americans in a variety of ways. In the comparatively short cultural heritage of the United States, the Civil War stands out. It was a unifying experience because the whole country suffered through it, regardless of what side they favored. It was a national tragedy and many historians claim that it was the event from which American nationalism and our sense of ourselves emerged. The Civil War (and in the U.S. it is *"The Civil War"*) is a concrete event which forms the focus of U.S. history in a way that the strung out and less coherent periods of North American colonization and the American Revolutionary War are not. Colonial America is a garbled cluster of Pilgrims, Thanksgiving, and the Salem Witch Trials to most Americans. The Revolutionary War, the French & Indian Wars, and the War of 1812 are jumbled together in our national memory as events of the Eastern seaboard including George Washington chopping down cherry trees, crossing rivers in the cold, and lots of men in wigs (not to be confused with Whigs and Tories). Mention *The Civil War,* however, and we have photographs. We see images of men and women who look real to us, though their dress and hairstyles are different. We know Gettysburg, Slavery, Lincoln, the Confederacy, and the burning of Atlanta. Most of all, we remember the battles and the romance of the Antebellum South. Physically, the Civil War is all around us, at least those in the Eastern and Midwestern portions of the U.S., because this war happened on home soil. The Southern U.S. endured not only the war but long decades of Reconstruction. Battlefield parks, historical markers, museum exhibits, and local festivals all bring us fleeting yet persistent contact with the past not just in the East, but in Tennessee, in Missouri, and Louisiana. It was a momentous event that happened here—under our feet.

The Civil War is immediately recognizable in our collective imaginations, though we differ in our interpretations of events and their meaning. At the same time, the Civil War is the romantic past. Times were different then. *We,* Americans, were different then. The Civil War offers the reenactor both enough historical legacy and contact into today's world that it can be reenacted and enough cultural distance to let one escape into a different world. It is fantasy yet has substance and meat that can satisfy a need to connect in a way that is very real and fulfilling.

Assignments

I. Cultural Impact and Maintenance of Folklore

The Civil War was a formative event for American identity. Both Union and Confederate areas were deeply affected due to the sheer magnitude of the war. In the South, in particular, the Civil War shaped ideas of regional identity. The antebellum period, the war, and the social upheaval of Reconstruction following the war are the stuff of Southern folklore and shape regional cultural identity today.

Assignment A: The Civil War and Cultural Identity

How big of an impact does the Civil War have on your family? You may need to ask a relative like a grandparent or parent to answer these questions.

1. Have you ever been to a Civil War reenactment or living history demonstration? If yes, what did you think about it?

   _____

   _____

   _____

2. Are there any Civil War historical markers or sites near your home? If you can't recall, you can check local Chambers of Commerce, libraries, or City Museums. Describe the sites below.

   _____

   _____

   _____

3. Are there any reenactments or living history exhibitions featuring the Civil War near your home? Who sponsors and participates in these?

   _____

   _____

   _____

Name _____ Date _____

4. Do you have an ancestor who was in the Civil War? _____
   What do you know about this person? How did you learn this?

   _____

   _____

   _____

5. Call or visit an older relative and ask them what they know about your ancestors'
   involvement in the Civil War. Ask how they feel about this family character (proud,
   embarrassed, etc.) and why.

   _____

   _____

   _____

6. On what "side" or sides did your ancestors participate? How do you think this affects
   family feeling about the war? (Non-combatants count, too.)

   _____

   _____

   _____

7. How do you feel about your family's Civil War involvement? (If your family does not
   have a historical connection, please answer how you feel about the war as an "outsider.")

   _____

   _____

   _____

Name _____ Date _____

Assignment B: Reflection on the Civil War and Cultural Identity

1. How do you think cultural factors such as religion, awareness of racial sensibilities, modernization, and the current political climate affect perception of the Civil War and people's maintenance of associated folklore?

_____

_____

_____

_____

_____

_____

_____

_____

2. Which "side" do you think has more active reenactors, Union, or Confederate? Why do you think this?

_____

_____

_____

_____

_____

_____

_____

_____

Name _____ Date _____

II. Learning More About Civil War Reenactors

Assignment A: Basic Information

1. What events and time period do Civil War reenactors reenact? _____

   _____

2. Approximately how many Civil War reenactors are there? _____

3. Why is it hard to get an exact number of Civil War reenactors? _____

   _____

   _____

4. What is an **impression** in Civil War reenacting culture?

   _____

   _____

5. When were some of the first Civil War reenactments and who staged them?

   _____

   _____

   _____

6. What is **living history** and how does it differ from standard reenacting?

   _____

   _____

   _____

7. What is **interpretation** and how is it related to reenacting and living history?

   _____

   _____

   _____

8. How did **living history** influence modern Civil War reenacting?

_____

_____

_____

9. What's a **farb?** _____

_____

_____

10. What's **stitch counter?**

_____

_____

_____

11. What's a **mainstreamer?**

_____

_____

_____

12. What are some of the different types of impressions that Civil War reenactors create?

_____

_____

_____

_____

_____

Assignment B: Getting to Know Types of Civil War Reenacting Groups

Part 1: Memorial and Ancestry-related Groups:

There are several different Civil War interest groups. The oldest of these are based upon memorialization or ancestral connection. Some of these have a reenactment component, or did in the past. Nevertheless, they are quite different from modern reenactors. In this assignment, you will learn how to distinguish reenactors from other Civil War interest groups.

What are Memorial, or Ancestry-related Associations? _____

_____

_____

Confederate-related groups:

1. For the **Confederacy**, what is the largest memorial/ancestry-based group for men?

   _____

   _____

2. Go to their official website to gather information. When and by whom was this group founded?

   _____

   _____

3. What is the stated goal of their organization? _____

   _____

4. What requirements do they have for membership?

   _____

5. Look at the news postings and information pages. In what sorts of activities are they involved?

   _____

   _____

6. Do they have any reenacting activities? _____

7. What is the group/chapter of this organization closest to your area? What is its name?

_____

8. For the **Confederacy**, what is the largest memorial/ancestry based group for women?

_____

9. Go to their official website to gather information. When and by whom was this group founded?

_____

_____

10. What is the stated goal of their organization? _____

_____

11. What requirements do they have for membership?

_____

12. Look at the news postings and information pages. In what sorts of activities are they involved?

_____

_____

13. Do they have any reenacting activities? _____

What is the group/chapter of this organization closest to your area? What is its name?

_____

_____

Name _____ Date _____

Union-related Groups:

1. What was the **Grand Army of the Republic**? Was there a group near your home?

   _____

   _____

2. What did GAR do? _____

   _____

3. What are the **Sons of Union Veterans of the Civil War (SUVCW)**?

   _____

   _____

4. Go to the official Sons of Union Veterans of the Civil War (SUVCW) website. Write down their url _____

   Where are the nearest groups?

   _____

5. Look at their news postings. In what sorts of activities are they involved?

   _____

   _____

6. Go to the official site for the **Auxiliary to the SUVCW.**

   Write down their url _____

   What are the Auxiliary?

   _____

   _____

7. Where are the nearest groups? _____

8. Look at their news postings. In what sorts of activities are they involved?

_____

_____

_____

Now, how do the Union-related and Confederacy-related memorial groups compare in their activities?

_____

_____

_____

_____

_____

_____

Assignment B: Getting to Know Types of Civil War Reenacting Groups

Part 2: Modern Reenactment-focused Groups:

Groups that are primarily focused on reenactment and living history are quite different from those such as the SCV or SUVCW that are based upon ancestral connections. Reenactment-focused groups can readily be distinguished with a quick review of their websites and newsletters.

Assignment B.2. Information Search on Modern Civil War Reenacting Groups:

Look for a Civil War Reenactment Group whose focus is reenacting and living history. You will need to find at least two groups: one group that reenacts Confederate troops and one that reenacts Union troops. Try to find a group that has people reenacting *both* sides (Yes, there are many reenactors that readily portray impressions from either side, as needed.)

Group 1: (Confederate Reenactors)

1. What is the name of the group? _____

2. Write down their url _____

3. What group or groups do they portray in reenactments?

_____

_____

4. Where are they based? _____

5. Look at their news postings. In what sorts of activities are they involved?

_____

_____

Group 2: (Union Reenactors)

1. What is the name of the group? _____

2. Write down their url _____

3. What group or groups do they portray in reenactments?

_____

_____

4. Where are they based? _____

5. Look at their news postings. In what sorts of activities are they involved?

_____

_____

Part 3: Modern Reenactment-focused Groups:

Assignment B.3. Essay Comparing and Contrasting Memorial/Ancestry Groups with Modern Civil War Reenacting Groups:

Write an essay comparing the two groups, based upon both the text and the information you have gathered above. Compare and Contrast: How are the reenactment-focused groups different from the SCV, UDC, and SUVCW groups? You can compare and contrast reenactment-focused groups from ancestral/memorial groups by answering the following questions about each:

- What images appear on the group's website as illustrations?

- What criteria do they have for membership?

- What topics are covered in their websites and/or newsletters? (Write down the names and topics of the articles and news)

- How do their activities compare?

    If they do fundraising, for what do they raise money?

    If they do volunteer work, what do they do?

To wrap up, make sure you answer the following questions:

    1. Which group is closer to your original perception of Civil War reenactors?

    2. Does this information change your perception of Civil War reenactors? If so, in what way?

III. Interview Practice: What Do Reenactors Actually Do?

For this exercise, you will practice interviewing a reenactor. You can usually locate reenactors that are willing to discuss what they do at either a reenactment or a local living history exhibit (reenactors are easy to find at local libraries and museums for these events.) You may also contact a reenactor through one of the websites you studied for the exercise above.

(You may notice that you will be using a variety of question types; remember that you will learn more if you let the consultant talk and even answer questions before you ask them or in a different order. You can always go back and re-ask or ask the consultant to clarify the answer to a question. Interrupting him/her, though, to keep rigidly to your interview sheet will only alienate your consultant, so resist the urge and go with the flow.)

Record the following information about your reenactor consultant:

Name: _____ Age: _____ Occupation: _____

Where or how you located your consultant for interview: _____

_____

Ask the following questions:

What is the name of the reenactment group or groups to which you belong?

_____

_____

_____

Are you a member of any other historical or related groups? _____ If yes, which ones?

_____

_____

_____

Which was the first reenactment group you became involved with?

_____

_____

_____

Name _____ Date _____

Please tell me how you become involved with reenacting.

_____

_____

_____

What do you most like about your current reenactment group?

_____

_____

_____

Can you tell me how much time you spend in each of the following reenactment-related activities? When done, go back and ask the consultant to rank the activities.

Activities	Time spent (hours/month)	Rank by importance
Reenacting battles		
Living history demonstrations		
Practicing skills		
Research and reading		
Garb/costume construction		
Manufacture of other artifacts		
Shopping/browsing for materials		
Conversation with other reenactors		
Meetings/administrative or organization planning		
Educational or charitable work		
Other . . .		
Other . . .		

Name _____ Date _____

What do you think you get out of reenacting?

_____

_____

_____

What is the thing about reenactors that you would most like non-reenactors to learn?

_____

_____

_____

PART III

Theory and Conclusions

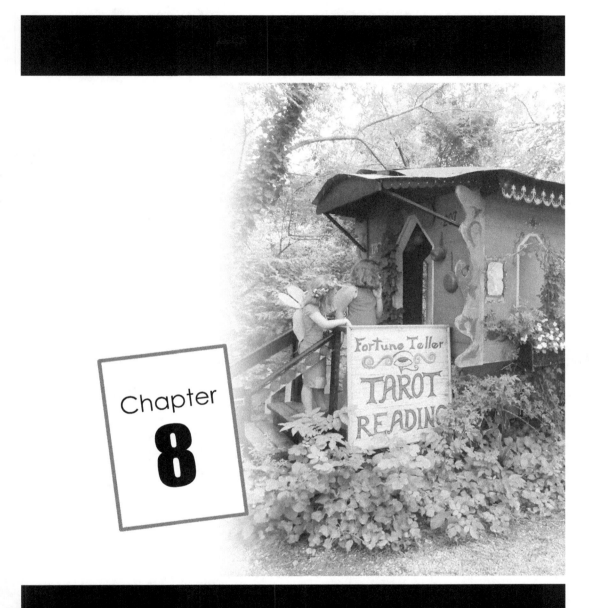

Chapter

8

Creating New Culture

Creating New Culture

Cultural Mechanisms for Creating New Cultures and Subcultures

The goal of anthropological ethnography is more than just description of cultures. The ethnographic data collected can be used to understand more about cultural mechanisms. The paracultures that reenactors create are fairly recently created social movements. We can use them as case studies to understand more about the creation of new subcultural groups.

Studying social movements involves understanding the reasons and mechanisms for the formation and continued existence of a group. Why/How do paracultures merge? Revitalization movements and invented traditions are two anthropological concepts which are mechanisms of culture change and the synthesis of new subsystems. Both revitalization movements and inventions of tradition are methods by which cultures may adapt to better meet the needs of individuals within a culture. Both concepts offer insight into how reenactment culture grows and develops as well as to why individuals participate. Together, the two concepts introduce a theoretical and anthropological way of viewing reenactment paracultures as social movements.

Revitalization Movements

Introduction to Revitalization Movements

Revitalization movements are cultural processes by which an alternate paradigm for a cultural subsystem challenges and replaces the current mode. A **paradigm** is a framework or model for understanding and thinking about a particular area of thought, especially for a body of knowledge. The *dominant paradigm* is the most prevalent or influential model people have for how a particular body of knowledge or part of a culture works. In order for culture to change, paradigms have to change as well, so these dominant paradigms are periodically replaced by new or updated paradigms. It can often be difficult to change people's minds, so paradigm changes are often accompanied by many debates and competition between people who subscribe to the dominant paradigm and the new, alternate paradigms being proposed. The cultural subsystem that is described or organized by the paradigm under debate could be a religious, medical, political, or other cultural system. This competition between alternative paradigms and periodic updates to how we understand the world is at the core of social movement formation and basic cultural evolution.

Because they are part of paradigm change and revision, revitalization movements are an integral step in the development and change of cultures from internal forces. Instances of revitalization had been known since early anthropological studies, but Anthony Wallace's (1956) unique grouping and modeling of revitalization movements changed the way anthropologists view both religion and cultures themselves. Although the most frequently studied aspect of revitalization movement is the process of replacing old systems for new, many revitalization movements actually result in the failure of the new system to be accepted. Instead, a reinvented, new-and-improved version of the old system or regains dominance, though it may need to update by integrating some new elements. *Revitalization movements are more about incorporating new or newly revised cultural elements that are more in tune with the current cultural needs of a people than wholesale replacement.* This repeats periodically, in a process that lets cultures undergo adaptive reinvention, editing, and updating.

In other words, just as computers need to update their operating systems to remain current and functional, cultures need to update to remain successful. Close study by Wallace showed that revitalization movements are actually cyclical, with three distinct phases in a cycle that repeats at differing rates depending on need due to stress within a culture. To learn more about revitalization movements, the concept of revitalization movements in the anthropological literature is reviewed first, then the factors behind and the traits typical to such movements is discussed.

It was Anthony F. C. Wallace who first assigned the term "revitalization movements" to provide a generalized terminology for a whole class of sociocultural phenomena involving deliberate attempts to innovate cultural systems (Wallace 1956, 1966). Most anthropological literature investigates the social process of religious revitalization movements. Indeed, revitalization movements are often religious phenomena, as people seek to reform a whole society from within through changes in religious beliefs and customs. Classic examples of revitalization movements that have been studied by ethnographers and historians include Melanesian cargo cults, the Mau Mau of Kenya, Mormonism, the Branch Davidians, and many movements among North American Indians, such as the Ghost Dance, the Peyote Cult, and the Handsome Lake Religion. Current examples of religious revitalization movements include American Neo-paganism and Modern Pagan Witchcraft.

It was Wallace's work with revitalization movements from the 1950s-70s that promoted the concept from cultural curiosity to being understood as a major process of culture-change. Wallace developed a theory of revitalization process with two major points. First, Wallace claimed that *all* the major religions—including Judaism, Christianity, and Islam—and their branches actually sprang from revitalization movements. Revealing the mechanisms of revitalization movements as integral to the birth and development of major religions made them one of the most important processes in shaping cultures over time. Before Wallace's work, revitalization movements had been seen as cultural novelties brought about by then-recent stresses like the European acculturation of "primitives." Secondly, Wallace described revitalization movements not as one-time events, but rather as stages in a regular, consistent cycle of cultural progress. The impact of Wallace's theory was strengthened because he also presented cross-cultural evidence documenting a uniform process for cycles of cultural change including these phenomena. It is the unification of all revitalization movements into a single class, with an overall mechanism incorporated into a functional explanatory model of culture change, that sets Wallace's work apart from earlier studies. Revitalization movements, according to Wallace, are a crucial step stage in an endless cycle of cultural processes. Since the adoption of Wallace's model, he and other anthropologists have explored many examples of revitalization movements. Revitalization movements, as a way for cultures to change or emerge, as described by Wallace and those who followed him, are now an accepted tenet of basic anthropological theory.

Before Wallace: How early anthropologists saw Revitalization Movements

In the early writings of anthropology, the technological "sophistication" of a society's culture and religion were used to rank its overall development and degree of civilization. Early writers in anthropology like Sirs Edward B. Tylor (1832–1917) and James Frazer (1854–1941) were unilineal evolutionists, believing that cultures and religions progressed upward to increasing sophistication. In this view, cultures (and their religions as a part of their culture) moved slowly upward through a linear progression beginning in savagery and barbarism and culminated to its peak in the "sophisticated" Western civilizations. In this view, all cultures were slowly moving and progressing forward but non-Western cultures were perceived as less advanced and definitely inferior. Cultural progression under this model was distinctly linear.

Franz Boas (1858–1942) and his many students introduced **historical particularism** into anthropology. In this new Boasian anthropology, "primitive" cultures were largely static, and their cultures were not seen as progressing at all, though they had a linear history. Studies of revitalization movements during these times considered to be separate events and defined by their specific, or "particular," cultural characteristics, each unique to their culture. Studies like Mooney's 1896 text *The Ghost Dance Religion and the Sioux Outbreak of 1890,* which described the classic revitalization movement among the Sioux in detail, were definite products of the Boasian tradition of cultural particularism, though the data from Mooney's book was reinterpreted and has been used by many scholars since. The Boasian tradition emphasized understanding a particular culture and set of events as unique, not as a process common to other situations or culture. Despite this, Documents and studies from this period have been useful because they have provided valuable ethnographic information for later studies. Wallace, LaBarre, and those who followed them in studying revitalization movements were able to use those studies from the Boasian period and before in order to perform cross-cultural comparisons and illustrate more generalized cultural processes.

Despite the fact that both of the early anthropological traditions utilized linear models of culture change, this early ethnographic work was still usable for reevaluation under the cyclical process model of Wallace. Both of the early traditions held culture change as a "gradual chain-reaction effect", a "slow, chain-like, self-contained procession of superorganic inevitabilities (Wallace 1956)." The result is that though Revitalization movements were recognized, they were seen as instances along that chain where rapid, momentous change occurs, (like the cultural devastation that results from European conquest and colonization) not as part of a normal pattern of cultural change.

The influence of Freud and psychology into later anthropology led to studies aimed at understanding *why* different types of revitalization movements took place. Scholars from the Culture and Personality era of anthropology such as Mead, Barnett, Linton, Williams, Smith and Wallis were all discussing different kinds and aspects of revitalization movements in the decade prior to Wallace's model. These studies directly influenced Wallace, and he recognized the importance of these scholars' work in his landmark 1956 paper in which he described his model of revitalization processes.

Wallace credits H. G. Barnett's, 1953 book, *Innovation: the Basis of Culture Change,* for its emphasis on acceptance and rejection of cultural innovations. The focus on the processes by which cultural innovations are either accepted or rejected was important to Wallace's model. Wallace was also influenced by Margaret Mead, who read a paper at the 1954 annual American Anthropology Association meeting detailing her work studying of **nativistic movements** (revivals of native culture in reaction to acculturation stress) with systems theory. Just a year later, Mead stated that cultures could and did change just in the span of a single generation, providing further inspiration for Wallace.

Wallace and Revitalization as an Adaptive Process

Wallace grouped the different aspects of these processes studied by other anthropologists into a group, and set about classifying and comparing them. In this way, he could better understand how these processes worked and how they were alike or dissimilar. For example, Linton specifically studied **nativistic movements**, which were a response to negative acculturation. The goal of nativistic movements is to reject alien elements from the culture in an attempt to purify and reinvigorate cultures (not just to change or replace the culture as other revitalization movements do). Even though Linton's research focused on a single type of revitalization movement, his work paved the way for Wallace's work. In particular, Linton proposed that cultural development moved forward and backward along a line of development. This was a new idea, since the dominant paradigm in anthropology before Linton was that culture was an ever-progressing straight line, with an emphasis on progress and forward development. While Linton's model was just a modification of the earlier linear evolution paradigm of how culture's evolve, it did accept that cultural processes could repeat. His idea of repeating processes was the first step in Wallace's idea that cultural processes could be a repeating cycle.

Wallace incorporated ideas and work from many other early anthropologists as well. From James Mooney's "revivalistic" movements, Wallace took the idea of instituting cultural elements, customs, and values lost from an idealized past. From Williams and Whitehead, Wallace added millenarian movements and cargo cults, different from Linton's nativistic movements in that they actively imported alien cultural elements and blended them with native cultural structures in an attempt to make a new, syncretized (blended) version of their religions. From Wilson Wallis came ethnographic studies and data on Prophets, prophetic movements, religious leaders, and Messianic movements.

Wallace credited the ideas and theoretical advancements in the work of all of these scholars for influencing his theory. What Wallace did with the field of culture change and process, however, unified all of these pieces into a coherent whole. Wallace stated that all of the phenomena such as millenarian movements, cargo cults, nativistic movements, and Messianic movements were merely different types of a universal cultural process. He termed this class of phenomena "revitalization movements" and set about describing a systematic model focused on process. Wallace's model of revitalization movements provided the hows and whys these earlier anthropologists had been seeking. It also transformed the loosely grouped category of revitalization process into a unified and widely applicable model for understanding a variety of phenomena as local variants of a universal process which cultures used to try to survive and adapt.

Wallace's Model of Revitalization

Cultural stresses that greatly disrupt a society—like colonization, invasion, war, large demographic shifts, assimilation, or relocation, to name a few—give rise to revitalization movements. The types of cultural change phenomena that arise are usually a mixture of several processes and depend on the cultural stresses provoking the movement. In Wallace's model, any particular type or mixture of types of the revitalization phenomena (cargo cults, Messianic movements, etc . . .) was possible. as members of the society tried to adapt and revise their culture so that it worked for them, meeting their needs. By accepting the different types of revitalization phenomena as variations on a theme, all with the same goal of relieving the stress felt by individuals within the society undergoing change, Wallace was able to simplify his model. The influence of Sigmund Freud's ideas from psychology and systems theory is obvious in Wallace's solution to organizing and clarifying the previously confusing and incoherent cultural phenomena as simply *"people trying to cope with stresses in their social environment."*

A revitalization movement, then, as articulated by Wallace, is **"a deliberate, organized, conscious effort by members of a society to construct a more satisfying culture."** The important phenomenological point in revitalization movements is that the individuals involved see their culture or parts of it (often, their religion) as a functional system. These parts, or subsystems, must also function. When they fail to function to the satisfaction of the people within the culture, they need to be repaired. People realize that they must change individual elements as well as the overall structure of the system, and they deliberately set out to build a new system which is better adapted to their present and future needs. It is the deliberateness and explicit nature of the attempt to update their culture that makes revitalization movements stand out from other mechanism of culture change. People within a revitalization period advertise and promote the need for change as well as their solution.

Wallace, as others in the 1950s before him, treated the revitalization movement as a response, an intentional emic adaptation of culture. Because revitalization is the process by which the people within the society are responding to the pressures exerted by their environment, both biological and nonbiological, it is an adaptive strategy for cultural evolution.

To better understand how revitalization movements can help societies survive, it is important to understand how Wallace viewed the function of culture and religion in societies. Religion and culture serve a vital function in a society. Culture, as a whole, is a society's extrasomatic, or nonbiological, means of adapting to the environment. It provides individuals within a society with "a design for living that helps mold responses to different situations" (Fagan 1997). In that context, a society's religious system, then, is the spiritual framework in the culture which helps individuals both psychologically and socioculturally. This explains why religious structure and change are so often studied by social scientists and why so much of the theory uses religion as its example. Other elements of culture besides religion provide people with cognitive or philosophical framework

SCA reenactors study details from texts, tapestries, and stained glass art to create authentic reproductions. Copyright Jupiter Images.

for coping psychologically and socioculturally, however, including the social connections for people in paracultures like reenactment groups. These ideas and the anthropological theories about how they work are used in this study because they have the common function of providing a functional model for behavior and belief.

In the Freudian- and systems theory- influenced anthropology of the 1950s, the rituals and experiences in a religion are part of the system which heals the discomfort and anxieties caused by various stressors, provides models for solving conflicts, and integrates individuals into a community. The myths and religious lore of a society provide models of coping for resolving conflicts, and the religious complex includes central values and behaviors that the individuals within a society need in order to integrate the varied parts of that society (Wallace 1966, Whitehead 1969). Cultural systems give individuals identities and placements within the structure of that system. People know where they fit within the system and how they relate to the world as long as their religious and cultural systems maintain a good adaptive fit to their environment.

The functions of religion and culture are exposed when stressors or shifts in the culture's environment change the needs of the society and expose failures in the current system. Common stressors preceding revitalization movements are political revolution, climate change, economic decline, civil war, culture change (such as technological innovations or an influx of new individuals), population decimation, invasions, and acculturation (see scholars like Linton 1943, Wallace 1956, 1966, La Barre 1970, Kehoe 1989, Haviland 1997, Kimbrough 1995). All of these stressors change the environment within which the cultural system (and its religious subsystem) functions. Inevitably, the now poorly adapted culture fails to meet all of the needs of the people within that society. These people begin to experience anxiety from uncertainty and the lack of a coping model within their cultural or religious system. They don't know how to act, what to do to improve the situation, or how to successfully manage. The society may decline, especially when in competition with other cultures. There are various adaptive coping strategies available to those within a society. One common solution is to consciously innovate their religious and cultural system into a new, better adapted model. Inventions of tradition, discussed below are often used to solidify new cultural elements.

Wallace's Cycle of Adaptiveness

After studying the Handsome Lake religion among the Seneca of the Iroquois, Wallace saw a pattern to the processes of revitalization. He was able to look at the hundreds of examples in anthropological literature and see common themes. He saw revitalization movements as adaptive phenomena instigated by members of a society to retool, or refit, their culture so that it would be better adapted to their physical, biological and cultural environment. Of especial importance to anthropologists is the conscious nature of the revitalization phase. The other phases of Wallace's cycle do not show this intense self-awareness, sometimes even to the point of the individuals within the society being unaware of the adaptive function of their culture.

Wallace's cycle is different in that it was the first to truly be a cycle, not a chain or line with only two points, or states. Instead of the old idea of a progressive linear development, cultures and their subsystems were moving through time with an ever-responsive functional process. Wallace proposed that culture is not directional or linear, as believed by Tylor and Frazer. It

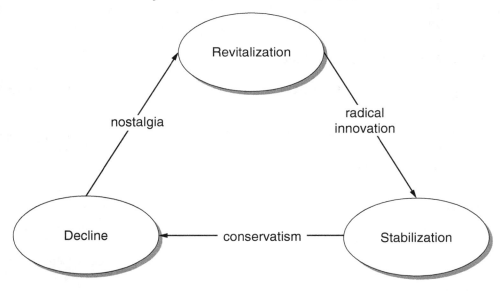

Cycle of Revitalization Movements

is not static, as treated by Boasian anthropologists. Instead, culture is adaptive, changing, and often cyclical. Wallace's cycle can be seen as a constant flow from **stabilization** to **decline** to **revitalization** (Figure 2.1).

Close examination of the three phases shows how the actions of a society reveal an attempt (sometimes consciously and sometimes unconsciously) to maximize the fitness of the system. The period of stable culture occurs when the society's cultural models are well adapted to their environment, allowing them to function and prosper in relation to their surroundings and neighbors. Stressors reduce the adaptiveness of their system, and a period of decline begins. The decline worsens until the society (or a portion of it) is threatened by their failure to function successfully. At this point, the society is ripe for a revitalization movement.

The revitalization period is typified by the intentional and conscious adaptation of the cultural subsystem to the perceived needs of the society's members. When a revitalization movement takes hold and successfully manages to innovate a new, better adapted system, stabilization begins. The stabilization period, in contrast to the revitalization period, is typified by a very conservative maintenance and codification of the newly adopted system. This helps to cement the new system into place. At this phase, any competition from alternate paradigms is vigorously avoided. This conservatism slowly shifts to nostalgia during the period of decline as members try to cling to the remnants of their tattered system. The liberalism and radical nature of the revitalization movement is necessary to loosen the hold of the entrenched structure on the past. Ironically, the separation from the entrenched system and a long-held pattern is to call for a move to an even more distant past. Often, the revitalization movement actually promises a return to the glory days of the distant past, nostalgically idealized and beloved system. The movement may even incorporate some of the symbology and ritual of the past. It is important to remember, though, that though the symbols are nostalgic, the system is newly innovated and is not actually a return to the paradigm of the past.

The Processual Structure

Wallace's (Wallace 1956, 1966) model breaks down the progression of steps that initiate the revitalization process. I have summarized his stages as follows:

I. **Steady State:** Most individuals within the population have their needs met. While some are under intolerable stress, they can be dealt with within the system without seriously disrupting others or the steady state of the system. Changes may and do occur, but they are integrated and do not upset the balance.

II. **The Period of Increased Individual Stress:** The individuals within one or more of the system's subpopulations experience stress with increasing frequency and intensity as the culture's efficiency and efficacy at satisfying individual needs both get worse. Many types of agents may interfere with the culture's efficiency, including; among others: changes in physical or biotic environment; military or political defeats; acculturation; economic distress; population fluxes due to epidemics, and migration.

III. **The Period of Cultural Distortion:** The individuals within the culture respond differently to stressors, and do not apply a uniform system. As a result, the culture warps, or distorts. The variety of coping mechanisms employed increases factionalism within the culture. Responses may include symptoms like alcoholism, ambivalence, infighting, abandonment of mores, and a variety of mental disorders. Various groups may make the system incoherent or piecemeal by trying to apply different, or alternative, pieces of behavior to "patch" the system. Mass disillusionment with the mazeway, or increasingly convoluted and increasingly nonfunctional system, increases the stress on individuals and the overall society. If a revitalization movement does not succeed, the period of cultural distortion may end in the death of the society.

IV. **The Period of Revitalization:** The culture is usually in a state of disarray, and has severe problems meeting the needs of individuals within the society. In many cases, it is on the brink of complete destruction from increasing problems stemming from the period of cultural distortion. Usual symptoms may include factionalism, epidemics, starvation, alcoholism, unemployment, and poverty. These problems may be solved or even forestalled by successful revitalization movements.

Within Stage IV, the period of revitalization, there are a series of predictable steps within the process.

1. **Mazeway of reformation:** Both the elements and the subsystems of the cultural system are restructured into an internally consistent structure. The mazeway, or path to reformation, is often dramatic, occurring first in a prophet or leader who brings others into conversion in a rapid, enthusiastic movement. The leader's gestalt insight is often a divine

revelation or inspiration. Hallucinations, dreams, meetings with supernatural beings, and visions of the future are the usual method of revelation. An apocalyptic problem is seen in broad overview, alongside a plan for restructuring society and averting the destruction of the prophet's people. The newly reborn prophet is often quite changed in personality and becomes a messianic figure with missionary intent. For examples of the dramatic conversion of revitalistic leaders, see the literature on such prophets as Handsome Lake, Jack Wilson, George Went Hensley, and John Slocum.

2. **Communication:** The visionary must then successfully reveal his revelations to people as a evangelist in order to become a prophet. He or she must convince listeners that the new way will do two things: protect and provide material benefits to both the individual and the culture.

3. **Organization:** Converts pick up the message with enthusiasm, often even with hysteria. The prophet must organize a structure to the new movement, often with deputies (disciples) to distribute the message to the wider base of followers. The structure must facilitate the spread of the message, provide a structure to shaping a new lifeway, and keep the movement going.

4. **Adaptation:** The reconstruction includes local adaptation to the everyday needs and function of the system. The new system as a whole must work, in general and in the particulars, for the newly converted society. In a pattern of feedback, the prophet often readjusts the message to find a better and better fit with the society. The new system grows and innovates until the fit is maximized.

5. **Cultural Transformation:** The new system takes effect as it is applied, reducing stresses and pressures on the individuals within the society. The better the adaptive fit and application of the system is, the better it serves it's newly restructured culture's individuals and overall society.

6. **Routinization:** The new system spreads and integrates into the overall cultural system and daily life of individuals. It's application becomes routine, and conservative forces hold it into place.

Stage V: The New Steady State

Once Stage IV is complete, the fifth and "final" stage begins and is maintained until the process is ready to begin again. The period of innovation ends, and a period of stabilization sets in, as the society attempts to hold steady the new system.

Revitalization and Wallace's Theory Today

Wallace's classification and modeling of revitalization movements is accepted and taught in anthropology courses today as basic theory. As it stands, it provides valuable insight into the processes that shape culture in general and religious movements in particular. Many anthropologists since Wallace have studied revitalization movements under Wallace's model, and it has stood the test of time. The goal of current research in this area seems to be to work out the nuances of the model. Recent studies (Anderson 1991, LaBarre 1962, 1970, Kehoe 1989, McLoughlin 1994) try to determine why revitalization movements took particular forms. The end goal is to have an understanding of the model that is not just interpretive but also predictive. After all, if Wallace's model is accurate, revitalization movements are a part of every culture and every religion, past and present. From the dawn of Christianity, Judaism and Islam to the Korean shaman dances of 1998, revitalization movements are born every day, often with tremendous cultural impact. Many recent fundamentalist movements, in particular, are revitalized movements with the potential to greatly impact world events.

Wallace's model is used in this study as a way of investigating and understanding the factors in the reenactment participation. Why do people join these alternative cultural groups? They are definitely participating in alternate paradigms of how people behave. The number of people involved in various types of reenactment have grown and participation seems to be holding steady, despite a general lack of acceptance by mainstream American culture. As several different types of reenactors are described in later chapters, they explain in their own words why they join alternative cultural groups. Prominent among their reasons, just as predicted by Wallace's work with revitalization movements, are the need for social participation and acceptance not available to them in mainstream culture and finding ways of coping with sociocultural stress that suit their personal needs.

Invention of Tradition

Introduction to Inventions of Tradition

Most societies have traditions, or practices, customs, and rituals that have been passed down through time, slowly evolving over time, yet providing a connection to the remnant beliefs, information, or wisdom of past generations. Sometimes, however, new social constructs pretend to be "real" historical artifacts or practices when they are, in fact, intentionally falsified for the purpose of manipulating public belief. The concept of invention of tradition is used to describe phenomena which societies (from the state-level down to social clubs) use to apply the authority of time-honored tradition to cultural practices that are actually recent in origin. There are two categories of invented traditions. The 'tradition' in question may either be 1) the product of a discrete, purposeful invention, or 2) a self-establishing yet recent practice. The concept is quite useful, not only for realizing that the appearance of long-time tradition may be deceiving even with many ritual-heavy cultural institutions, but also in pinpointing what the society-perceived was needed for cultural structure.

Eric Hobsbawm (Hobsbawm and Ranger 1983) is credited with developing the term and concept of '**invented tradition**'. In his definition, 'invented traditions' are practices which attempt to establish continuity with the past via new practices falsely given credit as being quite old. Invented traditions differ from other forms of culture change, innovation, and addition in that they are dishonest about their true origins. Unlike myths, which are also frequently ambiguous or dishonest about their credited origins, invented traditions are used to change cultural structure and performance. Regardless of whether they are invented as a discrete event or develop within a short, nondiscrete time period, invented traditions always claim time-honored authority that they don't really have.

The linkage to the past is necessary for the invented tradition to fulfill its function. The function of these practices is to repair a functional or consistency problem within a society's culture. Hobsbawm describes invented traditions succinctly as *"responses to novel situations which take the form of reference to old situations, or which establish their own past by quasi-obligatory repetition"* (Hobsbawm and Ranger 1983: 2). In other words, the invented practices are cultural adaptations designed to be integrated into the structures of the cultures undergoing functional stresses and stabilize them. They are "just so" stories that rewrite a historical cultural belief to suit the purposes of the person or agency who invents them. They are used to validate a particular point of view or version of history to serve as a false authority of time-honored tradition. If they are successful, they become common knowledge, and are seldom questioned versions of "how things have always been" in a relatively short time.

The functional stresses could be the problems created by changes, especially rapid or unexpected changes, that leave members of the society without a way of coping with novel situations. A new practice that provides appropriate behavior is invented or emerges through innovation then spreads and gains popularity as a meme. (A **meme** is a self-replicating cultural fragment such as a song, catch-phrase, image, etc.. that spreads through cultural transmission. For example, an individual "meme" image with a caption on social media is not actually a meme, but the practice of taking an image and manipulating a catchphrase to spread is, as is the song or catchphrase that makes the practice work.) If that practice is viewed as completely new or is not consistent with associated cultural practices, it may cause as much stress as the original disruption. Invented traditions, however, are designed to convince members of society who perform them that they invariable, a form of continuity with the past that helps to stabilize the overall cultural structure. Performing the new traditions takes or a ritual role. People like the consistency of traditions, and having a set of traditions to provide social stability makes cultures feel more stable.

Because invented traditions stabilize cultures undergoing functional stresses, they are often invented purposefully by governmental institutions, religions, and other authority figures such as political, religious, or commercial leaders seeking to cement and maintain their power structure. Carefully constructed or implemented invented traditions allow old institutions, like universities, governments or the Catholic Church, to maintain their stability to cope with novel situations in a manner that seems consistent. In addition, the new "traditions" appeal to people attempting to establish the validity of alternative paradigms or attempting to resist cultural change they perceive as threatening. Recently invented practices are repeated often to ensure that they are properly absorbed. People tend to forget the recent origin of invented traditions fairly rapidly (within a few years or a single generation) because they are oft-repeated and become common knowledge, unconsciously performed through habit. Because of the way societies remember, the new tradition replaces older ones because it is explained during the enculturation process as 'the way it's done' and often becomes established (and its recent origin lost) in a single generation (Connerton 1989).

A truly successful invention is a practice that blends so smoothly with the past or meets the functional need so well that its recent origin is quickly forgotten. For example, the very

"American" holiday of Thanksgiving with turkey, dressing, and family values is cited as a holiday originating in from early celebrations between English pilgrims and friendly east coast Native Americans in the 1600s. Children in our elementary schools are taught about Thanksgiving, usually with plays or stories containing "traditional" pilgrims from the Mayflower wearing black and white clothing and "Indians" who give the new settlers pumpkins, turkeys, and maize. This most traditional of American holidays, however, was actually invented and instituted in the 1863 by President Abraham Lincoln in order to increase a sense of American nationalism and family values during the stressful times of the American Civil War. Sarah Josepha Hale, the editor of *Godey's Lady's Book,* a prominent women's magazine, worked tirelessly to promote and "invent" the Thanksgiving tradition as we know it today. In addition to the countless letters she wrote to every official she could think of (including and especially the President of the United States), Hale published articles about Thanksgiving rituals, foods, and "tradition." Hale was largely success-

ful. Ask any American child (and most adults), and you will get the Hale version of the pilgrim story. American versions of Christmas, Easter, and Halloween are even more complex, with multiple instances of invention over the millenia as different religions and cultures assimilated these holidays over the centuries. Each gained new layers of interpretation, symbolism, and meaning each time it was appropriated and assimilated by a new culture, some purely historical tradition but much as intentional invention and rebranding.

A more classic example used in the development of Hobsbawm and Ranger's theory of how inventions of tradition function, however, is the invention of the Highland kilts of Scotland (Trevor-Roper *in* Hobsbawm and Ranger 1983). In particular, the clan-specific and short, distinctive kilt we think of today as a badge of Scottish national identity was actually a much-later 'tradition' born as a protesting response to Scotland's forceful Union with England that transformed the Scots' badge of barbarism into the badge of national pride.

How Revitalization Movements and Invented Traditions Relate

Inventions of tradition differ from revitalization movements in several ways. First, they are discretely created and distinctly discontinuous with their supposed historical sources is instead of being re-interpretations of whole cultural subsystems.

Artwork of royalty and knights provides inspiration for SCA garments and period accessories.
Copyright Jupiter Images.

The second difference in the functional level of the two items. Revitalization movements tend to be re-emergences of *concepts* and *beliefs* while invented traditions are *practices* designed to provide support and consistency for systems of belief. Inventions of tradition are actually the tools used by the proponents of competing dominant and alternative factions in the first four stages of revitalization movements. The dominant paradigm or institution uses invented traditions to attempt to cope with the cultural fracturing that emerges when people are dissatisfied with the current system. The competing paradigm uses invented tradition to give their movement the appeal of consistency, validity, and continuity with an idealized past in order to attract more people away from the dominant paradigm and onto its side.

For example, as cited above, Scottish nationalists used plaids as badges to assert their own history and nationalism in the face of acculturation by English culture after their political assimilation into the British Empire. Invented traditions that appeal to a group's desire to assert their "identity" are more successful, so they are often religious patriotic, or nationalistic. Another example would be the U.S. *Pledge of Allegiance*. I have repeatedly asked my college students about the tradition of reciting the pledge, and here is the common knowledge version: The U.S. *Pledge of Allegiance* was written by George Washington/Thomas Jefferson/the people who wrote the Constitution, and it has been said since 1776, with the phrase "under God." It is a true American tradition. This is a pretty consistently polled "fact" amongst this population. It is also an excellent example of Invention of Tradition used to cement nationalistic revitalization movements. To begin, the *Pledge* was written in 1892 by Francis Bellamy, not the Constitutional Congress of the previous century. Bellamy was a socialist, Baptist minister, and wanted to promote socialist and nationalist ideals for all Americans. He reportedly wanted to add "equality" to the pledge, but was afraid of offending men who did not want equality for women and African Americans. (Witham 2002, Robinson 2002).

The first published version read:

"I pledge allegiance to my Flag and the Republic for which it stands, one nation, indivisible, with liberty and justice for all." (Witham 2002)

This first pledge was an invented tradition published in a children's magazine, *Youth's Companion* to promote nationalistic, but socialistic ideals as a part of that social movement.

After the heavy waves of Eastern and Southern European immigration in the first two decades of the 20th century and World War I, a wave of American nationalism swept through the U.S. Americanizing immigrants was particularly important. In response, an edited version of the Pledge was promoted by the American Legion and the Daughters of the American Revolution in 1924 and was inserted into schools as a way to promote national identity (Robinson 2002). It became a tradition to recite the Pledge in schools and during public events.

After World War II, yet another wave of American nationalism swept the U.S. This revitalization movement sought to frame the U.S. as a world power, yet needed to reframe social life with a set of new "traditional" values that placed women back in the home (not in the workplace) and Christian idealogy against Communism as we found ourselves in the Cold War. As a part of this movement, called McCarthyism, the socialist roots of the pledge became a concern. The dominant paradigm of McCarthyistic American Nationalism held that Western capitalist nations were Christian, while rival Communists were atheists (Robinson 2002).

In 1954, President Eisenhower heard a sermon by Rev. George Docherty complaining that the *Pledge* sounded too communist. In his words.

> *"Apart from the mention of the phrase 'the United States of America,' it could be the pledge of any republic. In fact, I could hear little Muscovites repeat a similar pledge to their hammer-and-sickle flag in Moscow." (Whitham 2002, Baer 2002)*

As you can imagine, President Eisenhower was motivated to react, especially with national news coverage of the problem. Within three days, a bill was sent to Congress to add God to the *Pledge*. President Eisenhower signed the law adding the phrase "under God" on Flag Day, June 14, 1954, and announced that,

> *"From this day forward, the millions of our schoolchildren will daily proclaim in every city and town, every village and rural schoolhouse, the dedication of our nation and our people to the Almighty." (As quoted in Robinson 2002)*

His goal was to ensure that the pledge was both "a patriotic oath and a public prayer." As you can see, inventing a variety of public rituals and traditions, such as the *Pledge of Allegiance*, served to help cement and reinforce the paradigms of these nationalistic movements. They have been successful, as well. Most Americans accept the common knowledge "truth" that the *Pledge* is *and always has been* a custom that the U.S. has always been a Christian republic. Refusal to say the pledge, is still widely viewed as un-American, un-Christian, and un-patriotic behavior.

Proponents of both paradigms in a revitalization movement realize that cultural systems must 1) meet the functional and perceived needs of the people within the society and 2) do so in a fashion that provides people the assurance of stability. A revitalization is the *process* by which a society updates the *culture* as a whole so that it is a robust, cultural system for framing and coping with the world environment. Invented traditions are one of the *tools* with which this is done. While the revitalization process is usually the way in which an alternative or subordinate paradigm gains and cements the position of dominance, inventions of tradition may be used by either the alternate or the dominant paradigm.

While inventions of tradition are practices, it is important not to forget that they are also a means of justification. The cited distant historical source of the practice is its authority, much in the way that a reference citation in a manuscript uses the older, published reference cited as the authority, or "proof" of the validity of a statement. The ability to convince people within the society of their validity determines whether or not an invented tradition will be successful and durable.

While invented traditions can occur singly, they frequently occur in clusters of several closely-related practices. This is particularly true of institutions under great pressure to establish their validity. Often, smaller movements which fulfill only one cultural subsystem form close associations with other small movements with similar belief systems. The close interrelationship of Modern Pagan Witchcraft and Modern/Eclectic herbalism is an example of such an alliance (Chandler-Ezell 2003, Hutton 1999). Both of these counter-culture movements trace their roots to pre-Christian or at least pre-Industrialized Northwestern Europe. Both movements seek a closer connection with nature, domestic healthcare and a more female-centered view of history. Both are inconsistent with the other elements of Western culture. By forming an alliance, a complex integrating Paganism and Modern/Eclectic herbalism offer greater stability across cultural subsystems and make these movements more sustainable and comfortable for their practitioners. Similar clustering of invented traditions and revival of older traditions and practices is frequently seen among reenactors. For example, reenactors often learn a great deal about the history and cultural practices of their chosen reenactment genre and incorporate aspects not just from the clothing and hairstyles that are readily apparent to outsiders, but from multiple dimensions of that period into their daily and reenacting lives, including undergarments, accessories, culinary dishes or techniques, toiletries, traditions, music, and more. This gives participants a richer, more holistic experience. For most reenactors, the "costume" is not a façade and is much more than skin deep. They are often quite happy to discuss the skills, technology, philosophy, and even politics of their chosen period.

In summary, invented traditions are used to solidify a sense of group or cultural affiliation. Individuals gain, and, in turn, demonstrate their identity when they practice the traditions. Revitalization movements and invented traditions work together to change and shape cultures. Revitalization movements are the shifts between old and new paradigms of the culture while invented traditions stabilize and justify the paradigm with tradition, ritual, and custom.

Assignments

I. Learning More About Revitalization Movements

Assignment A: Basic Information

1. What is a revitalization movement?

   _____

   _____

2. According to Wallace, what are the types of revitalization movements?

   _____

   _____

3. What is a paradigm?

   _____

   _____

4. What is a nativistic movement?

   _____

   _____

Name _____ Date _____

Assignment B: Information Search on Revitalization Movement

Choose one of the following revitalization movements to write a 2–5 page report in AAA format. (You may choose another movement with instructor's permission).

Revitalization and Nativistic Movements

- The Ghost Dance
- Handsome Lake Religion
- Cargo Cults in Melanesia, Pacific Islands
- Rise of the Ku Klux Klan
- Terre sans Mal migrations in South America
- Hitler and National Socialism in Germany
- Gorbachev and perestroika in the Soviet Union
- Ayatollah Khomeini in Iran
- Peyote and Native American Church
- Black Nationalism in the United States
- Falungong

Report: For Your Report, You will Need to Provide the Following Information:

1. Author/ethnographer known for studying this movement.

2. What were the **dominant paradigm** and **alternate paradigm** in the movement?

3. The people and culture involved in the movement:

   a. The leader, or prophet starting the movement

   b. Supernatural vision, prophecy

   c. What the followers wanted

   d. Are there "bad guys" in the story?

4. The situation that prompted the revitalization movement

5. How did it turn out?

Name _____ Date _____

II. Learning More About the Invention of Tradition

Assignment A: What are Traditions in Popular and Personal Culture?

Part 1: Asking About Family Traditions

You may be assigned to either answer these questions yourself or to use them as interview questions to poll other people about this topic. Make sure you check with your instructor to determine which is your assignment.

1. How do *you* define "tradition?"

   _____

   _____

   _____

2. Describe 3 traditions that you (and perhaps your family) find to be very important. Be sure to describe the tradition and its meaning to you.

   _____

   _____

   _____

3. How long do you think something has to be practiced to become a "real" tradition?

   _____

   _____

   _____

4. Are there conflicts between different parts of your family on the "proper" version of a tradition? What are they, and how does your family try to solve the problem?

   _____

   _____

   _____

5. Is it really important to you to have the exact and accurate historical facts about a tradition, or do you like the standard pop culture version? Discuss the pros and cons of each.

   _____

   _____

   _____

Name _____ Date _____

Part 2: Invention of Traditions: Basic Terms and Concepts

Now that you have acted like a good ethnographer and talked to real people about traditions, look in your textbooks and do some background work on traditions.

1. What, anthropologically speaking, is a **tradition**?

   _____

   _____

   _____

2. How does an **invented tradition** differ from a "regular" tradition?

   _____

   _____

   _____

3. What is a **ritual**?

   _____

   _____

   _____

4. What is a **custom**?

   _____

   _____

   _____

5. Why do political agencies frequently invent traditions, and what sorts of traditions do they typically invent?

   _____

   _____

   _____

6. What are some examples (give at least 2) of political or commercial agencies inventing traditions? For each of these, how do you feel about these agencies inventing traditions?

   _____

   _____

   _____

Name _____ Date _____

III. Learning More About the Invention of Tradition

Assignment B: Researching the Origins of Popular Traditions

Assignment 1: Invented Traditions and Holidays

Research one or more (as assigned by your instructor) of the following invented traditions. Answer the following questions for each assigned tradition. You will need to cite your sources for full credit.

1. **Holidays: Be sure to think of typical customs, special foods, colors, and symbols associated with the holiday.**

2. **The "Hallmark Card Holidays":** Mother's Day, Grandparents' Day, Bosses' Day, St. Valentine's Day

3. **Patriotic, National, and "bank" or "post office" Holidays:** Memorial Day, Labor Day, Veterans' Day, President's Day, 4th of July, Thanksgiving (American and Canadian), VE Day *(note what day of the week these traditionally fall upon)*

4. **Religious holidays:** especially Christmas, Easter, All Saints Day, Ramadan, Hanukah, Passover, etc..

5. **Seasonal holidays:** End of Year, Solstices and Equinoxes, May Day, Halloween, Deer season, Boxing Day, NFL Draft Day, Super Bowl Sunday

Name of tradition selected _____

1. What is the tradition and/or how is the tradition celebrated?

   _____

   _____

   _____

2. What is the origin of the tradition? (From where and when did it come?) *(If there are supposed sources as well as real, historical sources, state both.)*

   _____

   _____

   _____

3. If a particular individual or agency "invented" the tradition, who was it?

_____

_____

_____

4. Was there an older tradition that was replaced or revised by the newer tradition? How/when did it change?

_____

_____

_____

III. Learning More About the Invention of Tradition

Assignment B: Researching the Origins of Popular Traditions

Assignment 2: Customs. Research one or more (as assigned by your instructor) of the following customs associated with invented traditions. Answer the following questions for each assigned tradition. You will need to cite your sources for full credit.

Customs & Rituals:

- Pastel colors for babies—blue for boys, pink for girls
- Scottish clan tartans and kilts
- Sending greeting cards/holiday cards
- White wedding dresses
- Wedding cakes
- White before/after Labor and Memorial Day
- Cotillions
- Traditional meals
- Bar and Bat mitzvah
- Quinceanera
- Circumcision customs
- Sweet 16
- Hurricane parties
- Wakes
- Sitting shiva

Name _____ Date _____

Name of custom selected _____

1. What is the custom and/or how is it performed?

   _____

   _____

   _____

2. What is the origin of the custom or ritual? (From where and when did it come?)
   (If there are supposed sources as well as real, historical sources, state both.)

   _____

   _____

   _____

3. If a particular individual or agency "invented" the custom, who was it?

   _____

   _____

   _____

4. Was there an older practice that was replaced or revised by the newer one? How/when
   did it change?

   _____

   _____

   _____

Chapter

9

Conclusions

Differences and Similarities Among Reenactors

Though there are many types of reenactors, this book focuses on three prevalent genres of historical reenactors in the U.S. While all share similarities, each is unique, meeting reenactors' needs in different ways. Civil War reenactors and SCA reenactors are more similar in their behavior, goals, and methods. Although Ren Faire reenactors and SCAdians overlap their time periods and cultures, they do not share other key traits. By design, the SCA is the most private reenacting experience, with most activities taking place out of the public eye in an "all-period" environment whenever possible. Civil War reenactors balance public demonstration with the need for private and authentic experiences in their quest to preserve historic sites and cultural memory with the American people. Both Civil War and SCA reenactors stress the need for historical accuracy. They are seeking an authentic experience based upon painstaking research into historical detail. By contrast, Faire reenactors revel in the loosening of the strictures of both time and reality to enjoy fantasy inspired by and only loosely based in historical events. Faire reenactors openly embrace public spectacle and consumerism yet somehow manage to find their magic amidst the mundane spectators.

All of the reenactors studied are seeking a way to achieve a state of sacred time—that liminal, shared space in which everyday social restrictions are removed. They all find benefit in the rituals and social networks build by their respective reenacting communities. The period rush reenactors seek is achieved in different ways. Faire reenactors create a festival atmosphere, where the cultural setting of a festival experience, role reversal, and loosening of normal social constraints creates the escapist benefits for both the reenactors and their spectators. Faire reenactors are processual actors, memorizing a script, accent, and relying on the freeing experience of being an exhibitionist performer. They revel in their festival characters in the loosened social environment of the Faire world.

SCA reenactors are seeking a time long ago in a place far, far away. Though many reenactors know they have ancestors from medieval or Renaissance Europe, most of them do not know the details of this heritage and are far removed from it in a cultural sense. SCAdians must recreate or invent a historical envelope with the help of others in their society. They are drawn to a vague and misty past that is different enough to be both fantastic and yet historically real enough to create as a very detailed, real alternative to their daily lives. The very temporal and geographical distance of the SCA genre is what makes it an escape destination.

Carnival and Mardi Gras are classic example of role reversal and the use of masks or costumes to be free of everyday social constrictions. Copyright Jupiter Images.

Because they construct detailed, long-lived, and very personalized personae, they carry the past and an alter ego who lives in that past within themselves. The SCA reenactor can alternate between parallel realities, moving into their paraculture when they need to escape daily social pressures or interact with fellow reenactors.

Civil War reenactors are different from either of the other types of reenactors in that they are standing rooted on their genre. While medieval Europe is a fairy tale land from the distant past, American land and culture is saturated with the recent past of the Civil War. Especially in the South and much of the Eastern U.S., Civil War reenactors physically encounter battlefields, memorials, and important historic sites from the Civil War. They are raised on family legacies that are close enough to be personal—grandparents tell them the stories of their grandparents, making the War close enough for deep personal meaning and fulfillment, but just far enough for fantasy and the excitement of an alternate reality. The Civil War is just far enough in the past to be the romantic stuff of folklore and a source of symbolic meaning for regional identity yet close enough to still be a source of heated emotional response. Antebellum homes, Southern belles in distress, and heroic tales of the war are culturally-important, iconic images with which many residents of the American South still readily identify. The icons and symbols of the Civil War are the icons and symbols of numerous regional identity movements. The Southern Identity movement, Christian identity groups, separatists/secessionists, and racial supremacy groups all co-opt Confederate symbols, icons, and language (Dentice and Chandler-Ezell 2009, Chandler-Ezell and

Civil War reenactors give a 21 gun salute in commemoration of fallen soldiers at a Civil War-era cemetery. Reenacting these rituals honors the soldiers they seek to reenact as well as providing a sense of communitas with other participants in the ritual.
Photo by Steve Shore.

Dentice 2008). The Confederate Battle Flag is a classic example of how these icons are lightning rods for controversy. Although it is an iconic image of Southern regional identity—even of basic American red-blooded patriotism for many—for others it is also the symbol of white supremacy and a reference to a regime that held a race in slavery. The Confederate flag has a polarizing effect on any crowd. Even when used in a historically-accurate way, the flag stirs up very deep emotions. Civil War reenacting has to deal with the residual race and identity issues of the War on top of the preconceptions outsiders have of reenactors in general.

Faire reenactors rely on the fun of dance, games, and recreational activities for excitement. Civil War and SCA reenactors and some Faire artisans and merchants can feel a sense of connection to their heritage and a sense of accomplishment by mastering skills and technology from their past. These sorts of activities are important cores to reenacting society, offering activities for bonding as well as the opportunity to achieve status in this new world. Status and rank in the Faire community is not based on mundane world status. The living history and method acting approach of the quest for period authenticity lets reenactors be deeply involved in both their escapism and their new society. Immersion and intense, climactic experience such as battle reenactments allow the reenactors to get lost in the moment and enter a different world. When they return to their mundane world, they often find that they are less stressed and better able to cope with the social pressures that await them there.

Reenacting, Ritual, and Communitas

Given the nature of reenacting, what is its function? The previous chapters reviewed misconceptions and stereotypes about reenactors. They are accused of being childish or psychologically deficient because role-playing is considered an immature form of play in our society. Adults are expected to maintain mainstream social roles. What the popularity of reenacting shows us, however, is that some adults need a break from their mainstream social roles. Several of the reenactors I interviewed commented that reenacting is an expensive hobby ". . . *but it's cheaper than therapy.*" Others simply said that when life gets too stressful, they "*need to play.*" Reenactors often don't sustain intense reenacting involvement, as "*real life gets in the way*" and takes up more of their time or resources. They often enjoy a good "*binge on a war*" or rewarding themselves by taking some vacation time and enjoying reenacting activities to clean out the cobwebs of mundane life or to "*reconnect with old comrades and friends.*" An important component of reenacting that makes it different from simply binging on a solitary recreational activity is that you binge not just on the recreation and escapism, but on a hands-on, tactile reality as well as live, face-to-face social interaction. Both of these dimensions can be sadly lacking in our daily lives. Reenactors are invigorating not just by the escapism, but by the connection to tactile experiences of reality.

Reenacting doesn't just provide companionship and social fulfillment through the paracultural community. Remember that it provides mental health benefits from the escapism and recreational aspect; reenactors can 'go there' when they need a break. For people who are experiencing very stressful mundane lives, taking on the role of a persona can actually let them switch to an alter ego that is themselves as they would be. Many of the SCA reenactors I have known over the years like their SCA persona better than their mundane self. More often, however, they explain that being their reenacting persona has helped them to become a better person in real life—that they have learned to take the best of themselves and of what they would like to be and integrate it into their daily lives. The alternate identity, however, is the start that lets them experience the positive self and gain confidence to become the person they want to be. It allows people to express their secret identity and meet their needs. "I *do* hear the cry of the warrior," quoted from Lt. Worf and numerous other Klingons from the *Star Trek* genre, strikes a chord with many people who engage in reenacting warriors and soldiers. It was mentioned several times by the reenactors I observed, often associated with a respect and desire to have a "Band of Brothers" or to live by the code of the warrior, by *Honor*.

To interpret it from psychological and sociological theory, we can think of reenacting as managed role play and impression management. Erving Goffman's *The Presentation of the Self in Everyday Life* (1959) and *Interaction Ritual* (1967) laid out the dramaturgical approach to interaction. His interpretation of why people enjoy reenacting would be that they can create positive impressions (characters) and then interact with others in a contrived social space that they have all agreed upon. So in reenacting, you and the reenactment community create a social space with special, desirable rules and engage in a set of actions and interactions with social identities that you get to construct as you desire. Reenactors get to negotiate social performances and interactions that they desire. It allows therapeutic construction of social action that lets reenactors rewrite themselves to be more of what they wish that they, and their lives were.

Masks and costumes for festivals are often fantastic or surreal to add to the sense of altered time. Assuming an alternate identity frees one from social conventions and everyday social roles.
Copyright Jupiter Images.

Reenacting paracultures also give people status for skills that aren't necessarily prized in mainstream culture, providing much-needed social support and acceptance. The social networks formed by reenacting communities are important mechanisms for mental and social wellness, transcending just reenacting activities and translating into friendship and social support in all aspects of their lives.

Managing stress and finding ways to be happier in your social group are important for good mental health. The strength of a person's **social support network** is a key factor in managing stress and recovering from traumatic events. People with little or no social networks do not manage stress or anxiety as well. People who are marginalized or who do not fit into mainstream society well often suffer from prolonged, increased levels of stress if they do not find a community or social group in which they can gain status outside of mainstream requirements.

Intense stress and anxiety can cause mental harm if the individual cannot alleviate that stress. Dissociative psychological disorders occur when an individual loses the ability to integrate social variables and reality, causing that person to dissociate, or "break" from their social role involuntarily. Often, these occur when an individual has faced extreme social pressure. Inability to escape from social pressure in a healthy way through other methods could actually cause a person to break psychologically.

Cultures are full of methods for mediating stress. Festivals, rituals, and communal activities can ameliorate stress and let the individual feel a sense of **communitas**, or bonding, with others in a way that vents social pressures. Performing **rituals**, repetitive or stereotyped symbolic behaviors, lets people communicate symbolically and expressively. Going to parties, dance clubs, bars, sporting events, religious rituals, and concerts are all common mechanisms for relieving stress or escaping stress through ritualized sacred time. Personal rituals using prayer, yoga, meditation, exercise, gaming, and music are also common therapeutic methods for moderating stress. Insufficient escapist or moderating behaviors can result in individuals accumulating too much stress, and therefore cause anxiety and unhappiness-a common complaint in our society.

Reenacting provides several mechanisms for relieving stress and alleviating anxiety. First, reenacting includes numerous personal and communal rituals that let the reenactor take advantage of the benefits of participating in rituals and the benefits of being in a close-knit community. The festival atmosphere of Faires is a straight-forward and standard cultural event that lets people enjoy stepping out of the constraints from their normal cultural roles. It is expected that people will "let loose" during festivals like Mardi Gras, celebratory parties, and festivals. Indeed, festivals contain ritual activities like dancing, parades, and the consumption of mind-altering substances to induce a mild **trance state** and create an atmosphere of sacred time for a large number of people. Rituals for individuals or smaller groups do the same by create a **liminal** or "betwixt and between" state for participants. Both of these are sacred times when normal social constraints and social roles are loosened. During sacred time, roles may even be reversed, allowing a sense of escapism that is very therapeutic. In Goffman's dramaturgical approach, sacred time is when we agree to constructed, symbolic presentations of different versions of ourselves in these ritual interactions. Reenacting actively seeks not only role reversal (through assuming impressions or personae) but also the bonding, or communitas, that is experienced by people who share that experience.

The Period Rush; Sacred Time for Reenactors

The period rush, described by Civil War reenactors, is a feeling of "being there, in the moment." They describe actually feeling the reality of the time being reenacted. Civil War, SCA, and Faire reenactors are able to lose their conscious awareness of themselves as their modern selves and feel like they are someone living through that event. They feel like they have captured the feeling, the emotion, and the experience of being part of the time. In so doing, they get a rush of exhilaration and bonding with their fellow reenactors as well as the actual people who originally experienced the events of the war. The period rush is a liminal state, a sense of sacred time experienced and shared with other reenactors.

This "period rush" is an interesting phenomenon that has been anthropologically described in other situations. For instance, a plethora of ritualistic activities are used in most cultures to achieve a trance—a state of consciousness where an individual or group has an experience where he or she loses touch with everyday reality. This transcendent experience can be an end to itself, leaving the individual feeling exhilarated, relieved of stress, and rejuvenated as a result. In religious ritual, the goal is to use this transcendent state to contact and communicate or at least commune with the supernatural. Many rituals are designed to give the individual a feeling of clarity by freeing them of everyday concerns or letting them obtain insight to a problem.

Public rituals guided by states, churches, and charismatic leaders create the mild trance-like effect called communitas. Communitas results in shared feelings of unity, bonding, and allegiance with others sharing the experience, with normal social structure, organization, and identity temporarily forgotten and replaced with the group bond (Crapo 2000). Skillful leaders can focus it to create feelings of brotherhood, loyalty, and nationalism while enacting rituals that relieve the public's stress, uncertainty, or anxiety. Even public sporting events are used to relieve stress and create a bonding experience between the audience members. The period rush, then, seems to be a type of transcendent experience where the reenactors loosen the stresses or constraints of their real or daily persona and as a result gain feelings of rejuvenation, relaxation, and brotherhood. Interestingly, the basic training or initiation phases of most military groups purposefully include activities designed to induce just this experience as a way of increasing camaraderie among soldiers. This culture of brotherhood among warriors is an important part of honor codes for many military groups. Scott Atran (Glausiusz 2003) has described how Al Qaeda training programs are designed to create familial bonds among members by placing recruits in small units and subjecting them to training exercises that create strong bond. They then use this feeling of brotherhood to take advantage of kin altruism, so that members will readily give their lives for the good of their new, fictive kin. The clever leader can use communitas for many purposes.

It is in the participating, the actual enacting of historically-accurate activities, that reenactors are able to experience the period rush. Having several people work cooperatively together intensifies the experience and adds both the immediate experience of transcendence and communitas to the construction of long-term group bonding with fellow reenactors.

What, then of invented traditions and revitalization? Reenacting paracultures are themselves revitalization movements, if not nativistic, then at least based upon deeply felt cultural identity and a need for a tribe of one's own. Reenactors have found a way to create a community that meets their emotional and social needs, sharing and giving prestige for the same skills, heritage, hobbies, and values that reenactors prize. They have invented their own traditions, steeped in the past they have reconstructed through painstaking research. These traditions help to cement their communities and give them rituals for dealing with stress and achieving a sense of brotherhood.

Reenacting allows people to spend time in a different social role, one that is chosen and constructed to the preferences and tastes of the individual. The time period or status of the characters being reenacted gives variety and an escape to an alternate social experience. It is play, but it is not immature. It uses the mechanisms of play, ritual, and festival behavior to achieve a therapeutic response. Reenacting is an adaptive method for coping with the pressures of our current social environment. More importantly, reenacting groups participate in several behaviors designed to create and strengthen social bonds among others, creating a social network.

The reenactor not only finds a method of venting pressure but also creates a new social group in which they have alternate ways of achieving status and interacting in a healthy way. In conclusion, historical reenactors have discovered how to integrate hobby, play, and ritualized behavior into a folk psychological therapy. They create a new social environment where they are happy and successful, then use that social network to buffer the excessive stresses of their mundane lives. Paracultures are parallel social environments that can absorb today's overload of stress. Paracultural behavior, from reenacting to extreme forms of hobby enthusiasm, could be symptoms of a need in our culture for mechanisms to deal with the stress our social roles place on individuals.

Name _____ Date _____

I. Basic Information

  1. What is **communitas** and what does it do?

  _____

  _____

  _____

  2. What is the **period rush**?

  _____

  _____

  _____

  3. What is **kin altruism** and how does it affect behavior?

  _____

  _____

  _____

  4. What does it mean to say that someone is in a **liminal state**?

  _____

  _____

  _____

  5. What is a major cause of dissociative psychological disorders?

  _____

  _____

  _____

6. What are some public rituals used to create **communitas**?

_____

_____

_____

7. What are some private rituals and how are they used to alleviate stress?

_____

_____

_____

8. How is Mardi Gras an example of the concepts of sacred time and role reversal?

_____

_____

_____

II. Comparing and Contrasting Types of Reenactors

1. How are SCA and Faire reenacting alike? (*Hint, don't forget to discuss personae*)

_____

_____

_____

2. . . . and how are they different?

_____

_____

_____

3. How are SCA and Civil War reenacting alike?

_____

_____

_____

4. . . . and how are they different?

_____

_____

_____

5. How are Faire and Civil War reenacting alike?

_____

_____

_____

6. . . . and how are they different?

_____

_____

_____

7. What are some overall characteristics of reenactors?

_____

_____

_____

8. What common misconceptions about reenactors are untrue?

_____

_____

_____

III. Graphing reenactors

Use the notes you took above to compare and contrast the different types of reenactors and use it to create a table or figure mapping out the different types of reenctors. What column headings would you use? How do they compare and overlap?

IV. The Function of Reenacting

1. What is the importance of a social support network?

_____

_____

_____

_____

2. How do reenacting paracultures enhance a person's social support network?

_____

_____

_____

_____

3. How does reenacting help people to deal with social stress?

_____

_____

_____

_____

4. How do reenactors use their paracultures to improve their quality of life?

_____

_____

_____

_____

Name _____ Date _____

V. Conclusions

1. How does reenacting relate to revitalization movement theory and the invention of tradition?

_____

_____

_____

_____

2. How does reenacting relate to the concepts of sacred time and role reversal in ritual?

_____

_____

_____

_____

3. How do reenacting rituals and methods explain the importance of assuming an alternate identity, or persona?

_____

_____

_____

_____

4. How are the alternate identities in reenacting key to defining reenacting communities as paracultures?

_____

_____

_____

_____

References

Abate, Frank R.
  1997 The Oxford Desk Dictionary and Thesaurus. Oxford University Press, USA; American Edition.

Adler, Margot
  1986 *Drawing Down the Moon* (1981, rev. ed. 1986). Penguin Books, London.

Agar, Michael
  1996 The Professional Stranger: An Informal Introduction to Ethnography, 2nd edition. New York: Academic Press.

Agnew, Vanessa
  2004 Introduction: What is Reenactment? *Criticism* 46:327–339.

Anderson, Jay
  1984 *Time Machines: The World of Living History. AASLH American Assn for State and Local History.*
  1982 Living History: simulating everyday life in living museums. *American Quarterly* 34:290–306.

Baer, John W. "The *Pledge of Allegiance*: A short history," at http://www.vineyard.net/ accessed 7/13/2017

Barnett, Homer G.
  1953 Innovation: the Basis of Cultural Change. New York: McGraw Hill.
  1957 Indian Shakers: A Messianic Cult of the Pacific Northwest. Carbondale, Illinois: Southern Illinois University Press.

Bernard, H. Russell
  2006 Research Methods in Anthropology: Qualitative and Quantitative Approaches. 4th edition. Alta Mira Press, Walnut Creek, CA.
  1995 Research Methods in Anthropology: Qualitative and Quantitative Approaches, 2nd edition. Alta Mira Press, Walnut Creek.

Black Confederates: The Forgotten Men in Gray. 2002. Desert Rose Productions. Documentary film by Stan Armstrong.

Borgatti, S.
  1998 ANTHROPAC 4.95. Analytic Technologies, Natick, MA.
  1999 Elicitation techniques for cultural domain analysis, chapter 1 in The Ethnographic Toolkit, Schensul, Jean and Margaret Weeks (eds.) Sage Publications, Newbury Park, California. at http://www.analytictech.com/borgatti/etk.htm

Boster, James S.
  1986 Exchange of varieties and information between Aguaruna manioc cultivators. American Anthropologist 88:428–436.
  1987 Introduction. American Behavioral Scientist 31:150–162.
  1994 The successive pile sort. Cultural Anthropology Methods Journal 6(2): 11–12.

Boster, James and Susan C. Weller
  1990 Cognitive and contextual variation in hot-cold classification. American Anthropologist 91:171–179.

Briggs, Charles L.
  1996 The politics of discursive authority in research on the "invention of tradition". Cultural Anthropology 11(4):435–469.

Canton, Cathy
  1999 Reenactors in the Parks: A study of external revolutionary war reenactment activity at national parks. Report for the 225th Anniversary of the American Revolution Planning Committee. NPS. Pdf available online at http://kingsown-patriots.org/parks.html

Chandler-Ezell, Karol
  2003 The Modern Herbal Synthesis: An ethnobotanical investigation of the emergence and function of herbal medicine in the revitalization of American healthcare. (Ph.D. Dissertation) University of Missouri, Columbia, MO.

Chandler-Ezell, Karol and Diane Dentice. The Klan and Medieval/Renaissance Reenactors: Religion and Ritual in Two Alternate Cultures. *2008 Proceedings of the ASSR-SW.* pp. 112–120.

Chavez, Leo R., F. Allan Hubbell, Juliet M. McMullin, Rebecca G. Martinez and Shiraz I.

Connerton, Paul
  1989 How societies remember. Cambridge: Cambridge University Press.

Cullen, Jim
  1995 *The Civil War in Popular Culture: A Reusable Past.* Smithsonian Institution Press, Washington, D.C.

D'Andrade, Roy
  1987 A folk model of the mind. In. Cultural Models in Language and Thought (editors Dorothy C. Holland and Naomi Quinn.) Cambridge University Press.
Dentice, Dianne and Karol Chandler-Ezell. Southern Cultural Nationalism: The South Texas Connection. *South Texas Studies 2009:* 53–64. (editorial review)
Franklin, John Hope
  1962 A Century of Civil War Observance. *Journal of Negro History.* April, 1962.
Gatewood, J. B.
  1983 Loose talk: Linguistic competence and recognition ability. American Anthropologist 85:378–86.
Garro, Linda C.
  1986 Intracultural variation in folk medical knowledge: a comparison between curers and noncurers. American Anthropologist 88:351–370.
Glassberg, David
  1986 *Time Machines: The World of Living History* by Jay Anderson. Review. *American Quarterly* 38(2): 305–310.
Glausiusz, Josie
  2003 The Surprises of Suicide Terrorism. Discover, October 2003, pp. 21–22.
Glory 1989 Tristar Pictures. Film directed by Edward Zwick.
Goffman, Erving.
  1959 The *Presentation of Self in Everyday Life.* Doubleday: Garden City, New York.
  1967 *Interaction Ritual.* Pantheon: New York.
Golphin, Vincent F.A.
  1998 Black Confederates have their own lesson to teach. About . . . *Time Magazine* (November 1998).
Hadden, Robert Lee
  1999 Reliving the Civil War: A Reenactor's Handbook. New York: Stackpole Books.
Handler, Richard, and William Saxton
  1988 Dyssimulation: Reflexivity, narrative, and the quest for authenticity in "living history". *Cultural Anthropology*, Vol. 3, No. 3 (Aug., 1988), pp. 242–260.
Haviland, William A.
  1997 Anthropology. Fort Worth, Texas: Harcourt Brace College Publishers.
Hobsbawn, Eric, and Terence Ranger, eds.
  1983 The Invention of Tradition. Cambridge: Cambridge University Press.

Hopman, Ellen Evert and Lawrence Bond
  1996 People of the Earth: The New Pagans Speak Out. Inner Traditions Press, London.
Hutton, Ronald
  2000 The Triumph of the Moon: A History of Modern Pagan Witchcraft. Oxford: Oxford University Press.
Jacobsen, James E.
  1997 The Civil War in Popular Culture: A Reusable Past. *Civil War History 43*:
Jorgensen, Joseph G.
  1972 The Sun Dance Religion: Power for the Powerless. Chicago, Illinois: The University of Chicago Press.
Keesing, Felix M.
  1953 Culture Change: An Analysis and Bibliography of Anthropological Sources. Stanford, California: Stanford University Press.
Kehoe, Alice Beck
  1989 The Ghost Dance: Ethnohistory and Revitalization. Fort Worth, Texas: Holt, Rinehart, and Winston.
Kimbrough, David L.
  1995 Taking Up Serpents: Snake Handlers of Eastern Kentucky. Chapel Hill, North Carolina: The University of North Carolina Press.
La Barre, Weston
  1938 The Peyote Cult. Norman, Oklahoma: University of Oklahoma Press.
  1962 They Shall Take Up Serpents: Psychology of the Southern Snake-Handling Cult. Minneapolis, Minnesota: University of Minnesota Press.
  1970 The Ghost Dance: Origins of Religion. Garden City, New York: Doubleday & Company, Inc.
Linton, Ralph
  1943 Nativistic movements. American Anthropologist 45:230–240.
Lowie, Robert H.
  1914 Ceremonialism in North America. *In* Lowie's Selected Papers in Anthropology, published 1960. C. Du Bois, ed. pp. 336–364. Berkeley, California: University of California Press.
McCurdy, David W., James P. Spradley, and Dianna J. Shandy
  2005 The Cultural Experience: Ethnography in Complex Society. Waveland Press, Inc. Long Grove, Illinois.
McLoughlin, William G.
  1984 Cherokees and Missionaries, 1789–1839. New Haven, Connecticut: Yale University Press.

1986 Cherokee Renascence in the New Republic. Princeton, New Jersey: Princeton University Press.

1994 The Cherokees and Christianity, 1794–1870: Essays on Acculturation and Cultural Persistence. Athens, Georgia: The University of Georgia Press.

Milne, K.
1993 Fighting a very civil Civil War. *New Statesman & Society* August 20, 1993: pp.12–13.

Mitchell, Margaret
1936 Gone With the Wind. New York: The MacMillan Company.

Mooney, James
1891 The Sacred Formulas of the Cherokees (revised and republished 1929 as "The Swimmer Manuscript: Cherokee Sacred Formulas & Medicinal Prescriptions"). Washington, D.C.: Bureau of American Ethnology.

1896 The Ghost-Dance Religion and the Sioux Outbreak of 1890. Chicago, Illinois: 1965 edition abridged, with an Introduction by Anthony F. C. Wallace. The University of Chicago Press.

Native Americans of The Civil War 2006. Desert Rose Productions. Documentary film by Stan Armstrong.

Nolan, Justin M. and Michael C. Robbins
1997 A measure of dichotomous category bias in free listing tasks. Cultural Anthropology Methods Journal 9 (3):8–12

Peterson, Kristen
2000 Black Confederates: Slaves or soldiers? Las Vegas Sun (August 19, 2000).

Rauschenberger, S. L., and S. J. Lynn
1995 Fantasy proneness, DSM-III-R Axis I Psychology, and Dissociation. *Journal of Abnormal Psychology 104*:373–380.

Robinton, B.A.
2010 "The U.S. *Pledge of Allegiance.*" Religous Tolerance: Ontario Consultants on Religious Tolerance. originally written 2002. revised 2010-FEB-07. accessed 2017-JUL-13 at http://www.religioustolerance.org/nat_pled1.htm

Romney, A. Kimball, Susan C. Weller and William Batchelder
1986 Culture as consensus: a theory of culture and informant accuracy. American Anthropologist 88:313–339.

Ryan, Gery, Justin M. Nolan, and Stanley Yoder
1999 Successive free listing: Using multiple free lists to generate explanatory models. In

press. Currently available at website: http://showme.missouri.edu/~anthgr/Classes/ANTH377/377.htm

Stanton, Cathy
2000 Review: Battle Road 2000. *The Journal of American History* 87 (3): 992–995.

Strauss, Mitchell D.
2003 Identity Construction Among Confederate Civil War Reenactors: A Study of Dress, Stage Props, and Discourse. *Clothing and Textiles Research Journal 21*:149–161.

Strauss, Mitchell D.
2003 Identity Construction Among Confederate Civil War Reenactors: A Study of Dress, Stage Props, and Discourse. *Clothing and Textiles Research Journal 21*:149–161.

Thrupp, Sylvia L., ed.
1962 Millenial Dreams in Action: Essays in Comparative Study. The Hague, Netherlands: Mouton & Co.

Trevor-Roper, Hugh
1983 The Invention of Tradition: The highland tradition of Scotland, in Hobsbawn, Eric, and Terence Ranger, eds. *The Invention of Tradition*. Cambridge: Cambridge University Press, pp. 15–42.

Turner, Rory
1988 Bloodless Battles: The Civil War Reenacted. *The Drama Review* 34 (4): 123–136.

Tylor, Edward B.
1871 Primitive Culture. 1:424–425.

Vener, A.M. and C. R. Hoffer
1965 Adolescent orientations to clothing. In M.E. Roach & J.B. Eicher (Eds.) Dress, *adornment and the social order* (pp.76–81). New York: John Wiley.

Wallace, Anthony F. C.
1956 Revitalization movements. American Anthropologist 58:264–281.

1966 Religion: An Anthropological View. New York: Random House.

1970 Culture and Personality. New York: Random House.

Wallis, Wilson D.
1943 Messiahs: Their Role in Civilization. Washington: American Council on Public Affairs.

Weller, Susan C.
1983 New data on intracultural variability: the hot-cold concept of medicine and illness. Human Organizations 42:249–257.

1984 Consistency and consensus among informants: disease concepts in a rural Mexican village. American Anthropologist 86:966–975.

1987 Shared knowledge, intracultural variation and knowledge aggregation. American Behavioral Scientist 31:178–193.

1998 Structural interviewing and questionnaire construction. *In* Handbook of Methods in Cultural Anthropology. H.R. Bernard, ed. pp. 365–410.

Weller, Susan C. and A. Kimball Romney
1988 Systematic Data Collection. Sage Publications. Newbury Park, California.

Whitehead, Alfred North
1926 Religion in the Making. Cleveland, Ohio: Meridian Books, The World Publishing Co.

Witham, Larry.
2002 *"If it says 'God,' so be it."* Washington Times, 2002-JUN-28 at: http://www.washtimes.com/ accessed 2017-JUL-13.

Young, James C.
1981 Medical Choice in a Mexican Village. Rutgers University Press, New Brunswick, N.J.

Young, James C. and Linda C. Garro
1982 Variation in the choice of treatment in two Mexican communities. Social Science & Medicine 16: 1453–1465.

Online resources and Reading Material:

Human Relations Area Files http://www.yale. edu/hraf. htm, database

The Authentic Campaigner, http://www.authentic-campaigner.com, newsletter

The Watchdog http://www.watchdogreview.com, newsletter

Civil War Historian magazine

North & South, a peer-reviewed magazine

Renaissance magazine, http://www.renaissance magazine.com

The Society for Creative Anachronism, Inc. www.sca.org

The Knowne World Handbook, Society for Creative Anachronism

Tournaments Illuminated, quarterly magazine of the Society for Creative Anachronism

Compleat Anachronist, quarterly pamphlet of the Society for Creative Anachronism